Emotional
Literacy

Emotional Literacy

To Be a Different Kind of Smart

Rob Bocchino

CORWIN PRESS, INC.
A Sage Publications Company
Thousand Oaks, California

For information address:

CORWIN
PRESS

Corwin Press, Inc.
A Sage Publications Company
2455 Teller Road
Thousand Oaks, California 91320
E-mail: order@corwinpress.com

SAGE Publications Ltd.
6 Bonhill Street
London EC2A 4PU
United Kingdom

SAGE Publications India Pvt. Ltd.
M-32 Market
Greater Kailash I
New Delhi 110 048 India

Printed in the United States of America

Library of Congress Cataloging-in-Publication Data

Bocchino, Rob.
    Emotional literacy: To be a different kind of smart / by
Rob Bocchino.
        p. cm.
    Includes bibliographical references and index.
    ISBN 0-8039-6823-X (cloth: alk. paper)
    ISBN 0-8039-6824-8 (paperback: alk. paper)
    1. Emotional intelligence. 2. Affect (Psychology) — Study and
and teaching. 3. Affective education. 4. Emotions in children.
5. Emotions and cognition. I. Title.
    BF576 .B63 1999
    152.4—dc21   99-6179

This book is printed on acid-free paper.

99 00 01 02 03 04 05 7 6 5 4 3 2 1

Corwin Editorial Assistant: Julia E. Parnell
Production Editor: Denise Santoyo
Editorial Assistant: Nevair Kabakian
Typesetter/Designer: Marion Warren
Indexer: Teri Greenberg
Cover Designer: Tracy E. Miller

Contents

To Kathy, my best friend,
with love, as always

Acknowledgments

There are so many people who have helped me on the journey that has led to this book that I cannot possible thank them all. Without them, I would have nothing to say; without them, I would be living a very different life.

I was raised in a household marked by alcoholism, neglect, emotional abuse, and physical violence; my mother was alcoholic. My brother, my sisters, and I lived in a state of almost constant fear and chaos. Our earliest memories, the earliest note that any of us recall, and the lullaby that we all learned in those most innocent moments of trusting the one who sang to us was the song of ridicule, of disgrace and humiliation.

Along the way there were people who made a difference for me, who helped me consider that there might be some other path, a path with heart.

So, thank you to my fifth-grade teacher, Miss Abercrombie, who taught me what it felt like to be recognized as a person. Thank you to Earl and Linda Kierstead, who gave me a place to live, when at 15, the threat of violence became too dangerous to ignore. And to Earl, who believed I had a good soul and invited me into the circle of caring. Thank you to Dave Sliwinski's parents, who took me in, and especially his mother, who for a short time I called mom.

To those who trusted and supported me, even when I was only as trustworthy as their faith in me created, thank you. Others helped me see what I might never have seen; to them and to Janet Donahue, thank you for that. And to the first person who taught me that I would be loved no matter what secrets I held, thank you, Betty Lou.

And to all of the teachers who helped me learn the lessons in this book, deep thanks. Bob Garmston, who, whether he knows it or not, is a model and mentor, and to Suzanne Bailey, thank you for sharing your wisdom.

And to my sweet, good, true friend, Bruce Bidwell, I am so lucky to know you; you care about people like no one I've ever known. You are just about the most generous person on the planet.

And to my sons, Dominick and Dante, who love me by choice and who have given me the gift of learning to love unselfishly, oh God, thank you. And most of all, with greater clarity of being and knowing than I have ever experienced in my life, thank you, Kathleen, my friend, partner, and wife. You have taught me what it means finally to love and be loved, to hurt and heal and stay committed to one truth. You make me want to be better than I am. You have taught me to believe and to have faith in love and to want to be loved, and there is no greater gift . . .

The contributions of the following reviewers are gratefully acknowledged:

TERRI LAWSON, Teacher
Tusculum View School
Greeneville, TN

SARAH NELSON, Principal
Houston Elementary School
Austin, TX

AMY ENDSLEY, School Psychologist
Citrus County, FL

About the Author

Rob Bocchino, a specialist in human learning and development, is cofounder of Heart of Change; Change of Heart, Associates. His consulting firm serves educational, business, and government systems throughout the world. He facilitates future search conferences and also works with the change process at both the organizational and personal levels. He has helped organizations establish and support self-directed and collaborative work teams through process reengineering and restructuring. His seminars cover fields related to human and systems learning, communication, leadership, change, and development. He also conducts workshops for educators, parents, and teachers, in thinking skills, multiple intelligences, and brain-compatible teaching and learning.

He is the author of several articles on topics such as individual and systems change, mind mapping, and the effects of fostering intrinsic motivation and empowerment. He has taught undergraduate and graduate courses at the Institute for Creative Conflict Resolution at the Maxwell School of Syracuse University. He taught secondary English in the public schools of Baltimore, Maryland, and Liverpool, New York, and worked as a staff development specialist in a New York State Board of Cooperative Educational Services.

Introduction

For the past 12 years or so, my partner and I have been studying, talking about, and teaching some variation of what has evolved into a body of information pertaining to what has come to be called *emotional literacy.* We have worked with thousands of teachers and observed hundreds of lessons, and from that, we have come to make some distinctions regarding this "different way to be smart." First, and perhaps most fundamentally, we see a difference between emotional intelligence and emotional literacy.

The word *intelligence* represents for us the potential for emotional fluency, somewhat like the innately human predisposition or potential for language or music or sports. And just as in reading, there is a potential for linguistic eloquence, so too with emotional intelligence, there is a predisposition in all of us to develop emotional tools and skills. The difference between emotional intelligence and emotional literacy, then, is simply this: Intelligence is the potential or predisposition; literacy is the constellation of skills, strategies, maps, and tools that we learn in order to become truly emotionally fluent. And it is important to remember that young people learn what they are taught.

Track coaches teach athletes how to run because they know that the way people "naturally" run is not effective when compared to the techniques of the trained sprinter or cross-country runner. So coaches don't settle for what their novice runners come with, and good coaches have the expectation that running can be improved. They teach running because they know it will make a difference. And the same thing is true for just about anything we first learn how to do naturally.

What if we devoted as much time to teaching the skills of emotional literacy as we do to running? To be conscious of the needs of others and at the same time to manage the demands of getting a job or a project finished on time takes great emotional literacy. To be able to maintain relationships and to communicate effectively are basic skills in any long-term friendship. To be able to coach oneself through the difficult times in life influences not only our own lives but also the lives of our friends, family members, and others who are close to us. And yet in schools, more time is probably spent teaching running than in teaching emotional literacy.

And what is *literacy?* It is, in part, the ability to decode cues, whether they are the printed cues on a page of text or the subtle cues of interpersonal communication. Moreover, literacy includes skills for creating meaning and the ability to apply that understanding to our own lives. Also, literacy is the ability to communicate fluently. And ultimately, being literate must include a constellation of cultural and personal maps that help us to understand not only the world out there but also ourselves.

This kind of wisdom does not come naturally, and without help, what skills we do gain are painfully hard-learned. It is probably unrealistic to even imagine that students would be able to use these kinds of complex skills and tools during what are often emotionally challenging real-life circumstances.

And yet this is exactly what we expect of young people. We expect it in their cooperative learning groups; we expect it on their sports, music, or other teams. Many parents, educators, and students themselves are quick to decry the loss of sportsmanship, of team work, of unselfishness. Yet these skills are at least as complex as the ones that lead to traditional literacy. Imagine for a moment that we taught reading like we teach emotional literacy. What right would we have to lament the state of literacy if we never taught children to read?

The purpose of this book is to begin to identify some of the key skills, maps, and tools that define emotional literacy. The distinctions between what is presented here and what comes to many people naturally are sometimes obvious, but more often than not, these distinctions are subtle, powerful, and somewhat demanding. There is probably nothing here that is too complex to understand, but that does not mean that doing the things in this book are easy. Emotional literacy takes rigor and a certain degree of self-control. But with guidance and with opportunities to reflect on their experiences, each of our students will become more able to understand and manage their own emotions, and they will be able to communicate more effectively. With support and modeling, students will be able to maintain healthier relationships, and they will be able to create and reach specific goals and outcomes. They can learn to be more empathetic and responsible. They can become more emotionally literate.

On any journey, it helps to have a guide who is familiar with the territory. As you begin reading, know that you are taking steps that may lead a student, a friend, or perhaps a loved one toward a path with a heart.

1

Emotional Literacy

Foundations and Background

Contents

- Research survey of emotional intelligence and literacy
- Perceptions of need for teaching emotional literacy
- Rationale for teaching emotional literacy
- Overview of the remaining sections and chapters

The degree to which I create relationships which facilitate the growth of others as separate persons is a measure of the growth I achieved in myself.

—Carl Rogers

It's a familiar scenario at the mall or the street corner: a group of teenagers hanging out, loud, dressed to send a message, waiting for something to happen. Two middle-aged couples on their way to the movies or shopping. As the two groups get closer, the tension rises. Eyes lock or shy away. The adults are afraid. The teenagers are disrespectful. Everyone gets a little tenser. No one speaks.

In a 1997 Public Agenda publication, *Kids These Days: What Americans Really Think About the Next Generation,* Farkas and Johnson (1997) cite a number of studies and surveys to paint an alarming picture of how adults and teens feel about the emotional development of young people today:

> Throughout this book, I will use icons and symbols to help you find key information, to provide additional comments and ideas regarding various topics, and to signal just what topics I am exploring. You can think of these images as signposts, anchors, or hypertext links to help you know where you're going and also to help you stay connected along the way.

> Whenever you see this kind of box, you will see definitions, technical information, and other kinds of specific research that may be interesting for further study.

When asked what first comes to mind when they think of today's teenager,

- Two thirds of Americans (67%) immediately reach for negative adjectives, such as "rude," "irresponsible," and "wild."
- Only 12% of parents with teens say they are friendly and helpful, and only 9% say they treat people with respect.
- More than 6 in 10 adults (61%) think that youngsters' failure to learn . . . honesty, respect and responsibility is a very serious problem.

Ask Americans to pick one overriding national concern, and chances are good they will pick kids. More than half of Americans surveyed (52%) think that helping youngsters get a good start in life ought to be society's most important goal.

And it's not just teens. According to Farkas and Johnson (1997), "Americans have surprisingly harsh things to say about younger children" [defined in their study as between the ages of 5 and 12]:

- When asked the first thing that comes to mind, 53% offered negative descriptions.

Some of the icons will represent key ideas and will be introduced along the way. For now, there is just one more that you should know about: The Factoid Sheet.

- Only 37% of Americans believe that "today's children . . . will make this country a better place" (p. 8).

- By an almost 2-to-1 margin (63% to 32%), Americans believe that "most parents face times when they really need help raising their kids" (p. 9).

Young people also feel something is needed. A recent Gallup Youth Survey (Gallup & Plump, 1995) shows a "whopping 96% of teens believe lessons in honesty should be a part of their regular curriculum. Another 92% feel that the curriculum should include lessons in caring" (p. 4). Some 88% support instruction in moral courage; 92% believe schools should teach tolerance. Overall, young people understand that something is missing, too. And they are looking to schools as a place to learn what they will need in order to be successful in the future.

FACTOID This is a factoid sheet. When you see one of these, you can expect an interesting, funny, or unusual bit of information or research.

What they need for their future has been outlined in a number of reports. One report published by the Secretary's Commission on Achieving Necessary Skills (SCANS; U.S. Department of Labor, 1990), identified "Workplace Know-How" as containing five competencies and a three-part foundation of skills and personal qualities that are needed for success.

SCANS is an acronym for the Secretary's Commission on Achieving Necessary Skills (1990), and it is based on research done by the United States Department of Labor.

The three-part foundation includes basic skills, thinking skills, and *personal qualities*. Emotional literacy is a fundamental foundation, then, to the Commission's recommendation. These personal qualities include responsibility, self-esteem, sociability, self-management, and integrity and honesty. In addition to this foundation, the report identifies another level of development necessary for success. These are *competencies*, defined in part as the ability to identify, organize, plan, and allocate resources, including time, money, and human resources. Other competencies reflect the importance of communication skills, interpersonal skills, the ability to acquire and use information, and the ability to understand complex interrelations. Another report, *Workplace Basics: The Skills Employers Want*, published by the Association for Supervision and Curriculum Development (1996), identified the following key workplace skill groups:

> The SCANS are divided into two broad categories:
> - Foundation Skills
>   - ✓ Basic skills—Problem solving, decision making
>   - ✓ Personal qualities
> - Competencies
>   - ✓ Managing resources
>   - ✓ Interpersonal skills
>   - ✓ Using information
>   - ✓ Systems thinking
>   - ✓ Technology

- Learning how to learn
- Communication skills: Speaking and listening effectively
- Adaptability skills: Solving problems and thinking creatively
- Developmental skills: Managing personal and professional growth
- Group effectiveness skills: Working with others
- Influencing skills: Making a difference

Again, there is a clearly articulated need for helping young people develop the skills and competencies of emotional literacy. In another book, *Emotional Intelligence*, Daniel Goleman (1995) puts it simply:

Emotional life is a domain that, as surely as math or reading, can be handled with greater or lesser skill, and requires its unique set of competencies. And how adept a person is at those is crucial to understanding why one person thrives in life, whereas another, of equal intellect, dead ends: Emotional aptitude is a *meta-ability*, determining how well we can use whatever other skills we have, including raw intellect. (p. 83)

In other words, a person's emotional literacy is a key factor in determining and predicting future success in any aspect of life and in all types of success. The ability to understand and manage emotions resourcefully, to communicate effectively, and to self-coach are essential for all of us.

So what if all of these concerns and demands for emotional intelligence could be met? What difference would it make? Could the familiar scene described earlier be avoided? Could a deeper self-understanding and control lead to richer interpersonal relationships, more fluent communications, and happier lives? Yes, it is possible. In fact, researchers are zeroing in on the specifics of emotional literacy, and in some schools, the interventions are yielding significant, long-term positive effects.

> A *meta-ability* represents a higher-order thinking or problem-solving skill. It is the ability to be self-aware and to practice self-management. It is an executive skill of assessing a situation, identifying approaches to reach a desired outcome, and organizing the actions to reach that goal.

Moreover, the very nature of these positive interventions is changing dramatically. In the past, much of the work was focused on what had gone wrong in an individual's past. This retrospective approach, by its very nature, is often reactive and focused on the behavior of individuals who were behaving in ways that were unhealthy or at least counterproductive. As a result, researchers have created an excellent catalog of dysfunctional patterns and have explored the root causes of many dysfunctions. Although there is certainly much to be said for a therapeutic approach that brings to consciousness unresolved issues from a person's past, this approach has largely ignored the patterns of behavior that successful individuals have displayed in response to the same kinds of causes that lead others to dysfunction. In their book *Competence, Courage and Change*, Waters and Lawrence (1993) explain, "with few exceptions, no vocabulary or armamentarium was developed to help . . . look at healthy processes, successful adaption, or personal resources" (p. 59).

The approach Waters and Lawrence (1993) outline examines the *successful* approaches, adaptations, skills, and behaviors of those effectively striving for mastery and growth. The manifestation of these skills and behaviors is seen as a means for developing proactive inter-

FACTOID

There are many good reasons for studying the causes and consequences of dysfunctional behavior, but this is only one approach. The study of those who succeed in spite of difficulty is sometimes referred to as the study of *personal resiliency*. Instead of focusing on what has gone wrong, researchers in this area work to isolate those behaviors that lead to success.

ventions that are applicable to anyone interested in enhancing competence and emotional literacy in themselves or others.

The purpose of this book is to provide educators, parents, and others with means of learning about the kinds of interventions that work. To best support that learning, the book is divided into five sections:

1. Overview and Background of Emotional Literacy
2. Understanding and Managing Emotion
3. Effective Communication Skills and Rapport Building
4. Developing an Internal Coach
5. Implications and Possibilities for the Future

Overview and background of emotional literacy. In this first section, Chapters 1 and 2, the book examines aspects of emotional literacy itself. We will explore what different researchers are saying about the domain of emotional intelligence. And we will answer some questions: What are the three broad areas of competency? What are the specific skills and abilities within each of the broad areas? What results have been found as an outcome of focusing on emotional literacy in schools? What does it mean to be emotionally literate?

Understanding and managing emotion is the focus of the second section, Chapters 3 and 4. This section will serve as a framework for educators, parents, and others to explore one of these three broad areas of competency:

- Understanding the *triune brain*
- Managing emotion in self —*Anchoring*

- Creating resource states —
  *Reframing and positive
  intentionality*

This section will also describe the kinds of activities educators can use in their buildings and classrooms. Parents or other adults might also (with some adjustments) use them in their homes and personal lives. In any case, this section will provide specific skills and activities to foster the development of greater emotional literacy.

Effective communication skills and rapport building are the focus of the third section. Chapters 5 through 8 present the four key topics of this section, which include

- Reflective listening
- Overcoming reactive responses
- Decoding nonverbal cues
- Assertion skills

Peter Asher, a University of Illinois psychologist, has designed a series of "friendship coaching" sessions for unpopular children. Identifying third and fourth graders who were the least liked in their classes, Asher gave them six sessions in how to "make playing games more fun" through being "friendly, fun, and nice" (p. 251).

The coaching had a remarkable success: "a year later, the children who were coached—all of whom were selected because they were the least liked in their class—were now solidly in the middle of classroom popularity. None were stars, but none were rejects" (Goleman, 1995, p. 252).

In this section, there are suggestions for activities and lessons for developing strong communication skills.

Developing an internal coach is the emphasis of Chapters 9, 10, and 11. This section concentrates on

- Learning from experience
- Creating a precise vision
- Fostering efficacy

Implications and possibilities for the future is the topic for the last chapter. In it, we explore some of the broad implications of integrating

FACTOID Joan Borysenko, PhD, helped found the Mind/Body Clinic at the Harvard Medical School and has worked with more than 2000 patients there. Her work has helped thousands lead happier, healthier lives as a result of their learning to manage their emotions in more useful ways.

emotional literacy into schools and communities. What are the possibilities for next steps? How will our first steps lead to deeper understandings? What are the future plans? And what might that future look like?

And just what might that future look like? According to Borysenko (1987), it could even translate to better health. "Recent major studies indicate that approximately seventy-five percent of visits to the doctor are either for illnesses that get better by themselves, or for disorders related to anxiety and stress" (p. 89). She goes on to point out that the part of the brain that controls emotion "has receptor sites for molecules produced by the immune system . . . a pathway through which our emotions . . . can affect the body's ability to defend itself [from disease]" (pp. 90-91). Other researchers (e.g., Caine & Caine, 1991; Sousa, 1998) point to a future in schools where teaching and learning are "brain-compatible," where instruction begins with the child's whole being.

The brain is not divided into individual segments marked "feelings"

"The hopeful sign is that many or most rejected children can be brought into the circle of friendship with some basic emotional coaching" (Goleman, 1995, p. 252).

or "cognitive development" or "physical activity." Successful students have emotional repertoires that support their ability to use the other skills and strategies at their disposal. For instance, emotionally literate individuals, whether they are at play, at work, or learning, have capacities to deal with a psycho-physiological response known as *downshifting*, a fight-or-flight response that interferes with higher-order thinking and problem-solving abilities. On the other hand, downshifted students who lack emotional literacy lose much of their capacities for learning and creativity.

The future, whether we look from the perspective of school to work, school to learn, or from the tensions inherent in an ever-changing society, demands a rich complement of tools, skills, and strategies to support a high level of emotional literacy. In any case, the future of a classroom, or school, or of a family for that matter, that fosters emotional literacy will be much richer, not only for the individuals within it but for all its members and the community alike.

And it is the aim of this book to provide knowledge, skills, activities and resources to support that profound and robust future.

FACTOID In Chapter 3, we will take a closer look at MacLean's (1990) *Triune Brain Model*. His work sheds light on what may be some of the most important aspects of human emotional behavior.

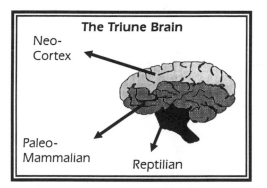

The Triune Brain

Neo-Cortex

Paleo-Mammalian

Reptilian

FACTOID The term <u>downshifting</u> first appeared in Leslie Hart's (1983) book, *Human Mind and Human Learning*.

Summary

As supported by research and as reported by young people and adults alike, there is a persistent call for the development of emotional literacy in our children. This chapter introduces the concept of studying the successful strategies that emotionally intelligent people use to enable themselves to succeed in their lives. Toward this end, the book examines five areas:

1. The background and research on emotional literacy
2. Understanding and managing emotion
3. Communication skills and rapport building
4. Developing an internal coach
5. Implications and next steps

2

Defining Emotional Intelligence and Emotional Literacy

Contents

- Research survey
- Distinctions: Emotional intelligence and emotional literacy
- Explanation of various perspectives of emotional intelligence
- Overview of three competency domains of emotional literacy

Intelligence without character is a dangerous thing.

—Gloria Steinem

Since the late 19th century we, have used IQ test scores to predict whether a person might succeed in his or her education and therefore, in his or her entire life. We have assessed this intelligence using instruments developed to measure specific responses to tasks or problems, and for many years, we then used these instruments to "sort" our children in schools. And though our experience and hearts may have told us that there was something not quite accurate or right about this method of predicting success, the question of whether we were simply creating a system that promoted its own self-fulfilling prophecy remained unasked.

Only recently have we begun to recognize and value a fuller exploration of what human intelligence really is. Researchers such as Howard Gardner (1983), Robert Slavin (1995, 1996, 1998), and Ellen Langer (1989,1997) have begun to redefine what it means to be intelligent, what there is to measure, and the nature of genius itself. And out of that research, a much more powerful predictor of future success has emerged. It is called *emotional literacy.*

Daniel Goleman's (1995) book, *Emotional Intelligence,* attributes this discovery, in part, to the brain research that provides a much deeper understanding of the link between thinking and emotions. We can also link this new understanding to the day-to-day evidence in our schools, our workplaces, and our society. Researchers find that people with emotional literacy are more likely to be successful—and that success is evident in their professional and personal lives.

Almost everyone knows of some cognitively advanced student who is unable to enjoy healthy relationships with his or her peers. Furthermore, we all recognize the power of an emotionally literate person who may not have the technical or cognitive skills but has the ability to understand relationships, to react to the communications of others, and manage emotions, using a broad repertoire of strategies. At least part of the explanation of the differences between these two people can be attributed to their levels of emotional literacy.

The term *emotional literacy* is a purposeful distinction from the term *emotional intelligence.* Emotional intelligence is the characteristic, the personality dynamic or the potential, that can be nurtured and developed in a person. It is the subject that Daniel Goleman (1995) and others have researched and defined. Emotional literacy is the constellation of understandings, skills, and strategies that a person can develop and nurture from infancy throughout his or her entire lifetime. Goleman and others have defined the personality dynamic. The goal of this work is to examine the ways educators and other adults can learn about and develop emotional literacy. It is my hope, then, that these adults will influence the development of the emotional literacy of children.

And so, just as with traditional literacy, where we continue to develop strategies and skills for reading, we can increase our strategies for emotional literacy as well. The strategies suggested in this book are aligned with the behaviors indicative of a person with emotional literacy, that is, a person with the ability to select and apply behaviors and strategies from a wide choice of options.

FACTOID

Dan Goleman's book, *Emotional Intelligence*, was published in 1995. The book provides an excellent overview and explanation of the research on emotional intelligence. Goleman is not a scientist, however; he is a journalist who researched and interviewed psychologists and researchers from around the country. Unless otherwise noted, the citations in this chapter are from Goleman.

Goleman (1995) points out the importance of emotional intelligence when he says that it "is actually a constellation of abilities, skills, and dispositions which, when taken together, can predict a person's likelihood of future success in a number of areas, including 'one's ultimate niche in society.' " This constellation includes (but is not limited to) "leadership, the ability to nurture relationships and keep friends, the ability to resolve conflicts and skill at social analysis" (p. 64).

Another researcher, Howard Gardner of Harvard University, parallels Goleman's (1995) thinking. In studying the different intelligences with which people function and solve problems, Gardner found two that are specifically aligned with the emotional, or affective, domain: the *interpersonal* and *intrapersonal* intelligences. He is quoted by Goleman:

*Inter*personal intelligence is the ability to understand other people: what motivates them, how they work, how to work cooperatively with them. . . . *Intra*personal intelligence . . . is a correlative ability, turned inward. It is the capacity to form an accurate, veridical model of oneself and to be able to use that model to operate effectively in life. (p. 39)

Intrapersonal intelligence is the sense of self-awareness that enables us to assume the third person, to observe ourselves, our emotions, our behaviors, and to be conscious of the insights we receive as a result of that observation. The two abilities, or intelligences, combine as the foundations and goals of emotional literacy.

Goleman (1995) cites another researcher, Yale psychologist Peter Salovey, who sees emotional intelligence as having five domains, which are closely aligned with Gardner's (1983) interpersonal and intrapersonal intelligences. Salovey (as quoted in Goleman, 1995) defines these domains as:

"1. Knowing one's emotions. Self-awareness recognizing a feeling *as it happens* . . . the ability to monitor feelings from moment to moment" (p. 43).

Emotional literacy is the ability to monitor feelings in a variety of ways. An emotionally literate person may be conscious of the physiological responses that accompany certain emotions; he or she may purposefully take time to reflect and record those emotions or may carefully track

> *Interpersonal intelligence is the measure of a person's ability to work with and understand others and to form positive, healthy relationships. Intrapersonal intelligence is the ability to understand one's self and to recognize the subtle differences between emotions, as well as the causes of those feelings.*

which emotions are present at which times or circumstances of his or her daily life. This self-awareness is the necessary step toward managing emotions in a useful way.

"2. *Managing emotions.* Handling feelings so they are appropriate is an ability that builds on self-awareness." (Salovey, as quoted in Goleman, 1995, p. 43).

This domain includes the fundamental ability to self-coach in order to manage the recognized emotions. Developing an inner coach to suggest strategies, to weigh the consequences of our behaviors, and to encourage resourceful responses is a critical skill in building literacy. The child in a classroom who can actually identify her feelings of frustration around some task, weigh several choices and their appropriateness, and manage (through self talk) to proceed in a useful way will not only find success in completing the task, but also develop a sense of efficacy around her emotional behaviors as well. The parent who talks out loud about what his choices may be in handling a difficult situation with his child, models his self coaching and the concept of a variety of conscious choices for those around him.

"3. *Motivating oneself,* marshaling emotions in the service of a goal, emotional self-control delaying gratification and stifling impulsiveness" (Goleman, 1995, p. 43).

A *meta-ability* represents a higher-order thinking or problem-solving skill. It is the ability to be self-aware and to practice self-management. It is an executive skill of assessing a situation, identifying approaches to reach a desired outcome, and organizing the actions to reach that goal.

Again, this is a self-coaching area that requires intrinsic rather than extrinsic motivation. Although we can create a temporary state of extrinsic motivation, it is the development of the personality characteristic of intrinsic motivation that is a key to emotional literacy. Educators aware of creating this characteristic can use praise appropriately to enhance the belief that the success or failure of the student is linked to his or her effort rather than to some outside force.

Dr. Arthur Costa (1991), in *The School as a Home for the Mind*, identifies *decreasing impulsivity* as an indicator of intelligent behavior. An emotionally literate person is consciously aware of the possibility of impulsivity, has a variety of ways of monitoring his or her own behavior for impulsiveness, and is able to develop strategies and plans to manage the problem or task at hand.

> "4. *Recognizing emotions in others.* Empathy . . . is the fundamental 'people skill.' People who are empathetic are more attuned to the subtle social signals that indicate what others need or want" (Salovey, as quoted in Goleman, 1995, p. 44).

Highly developed sensory acuity, the ability to read nonverbal messages, is fundamental to recognizing emotions in others. Deborah Tannen (1990, 1994, 1998) and others estimate that 90% or more of our communication and emotional overlays are expressed nonverbally. Receiving, interpreting, and responding to such significant communication are skills that most children begin to develop as infants in answer to their parents' modeling and responses. These skills can become more conscious, more developed, and more accessible (even at highly emotional times) when a person purposefully adds them to his strategies and behaviors.

> "5. *Handling relationships.* The art of relationships is, in large part, skill in managing emotions in others" (Salovey, as quoted in Goleman, 1995, p. 44).

Effective listening, high-level communication skills (nonverbals again), expressing emotion appropriately, and the skills of negotiating solutions are fundamental to this domain.

Piaget identifies truly effective listening as the highest form of intelligence. This ability to truly understand, without filtering or prejudging what another is saying, is a cornerstone in managing relationships and emotions. Emotional literacy demands that a person learn to be aware of his or her own filters that may distort a communication. It requires that he or she practice strategies to eliminate or lessen these filters. It provides him or her with good listening strategies, including paraphrasing and reflective listening. With careful listening, a person can accurately communicate and understand so that he or she is able to maintain and nurture the relationship.

Other relationship skills contribute to this domain. Possessing a variety of negotiation strategies, agreement-setting models, and social and rapport-building skills all fall into the realm of handling relationships.

In the classroom, educators can model listening strategies from the simple to the complex. They can provide opportunities and time to teach and practice negotiation strategies. They can have students consciously process the use and the effects of these strategies in their own relationships. Certainly, cooperative learning and higher-order-thinking classroom cultures inherently invite such learning and teaching. Faculty meetings provide opportunities for individuals to practice; parent conferences and site-based decision making could be enhanced by the conscious development of the skills of listening.

The good news is that emotional literacy can be introduced and nurtured throughout a lifetime. Children (and adults) who may lack appropriate modeling at home can develop literacy in school. Teenagers struggling with limited strategies in dealing with mounting problems and pressures can be taught a repertoire of techniques to make them conscious and give them choices. We can, as educators and parents, model emotional literacy and provide practical strategies and support. Although, it is true, as Goleman (1995) notes, that "such interventions work best when they trace the emotional timetable of development" (p. 121), there is also evidence that efforts at any time in a person's development can increase the emotional literacy—the conscious choices available to a person.

In recognizing the many researchers and models available, I will approach the information and strategies using a framework focusing

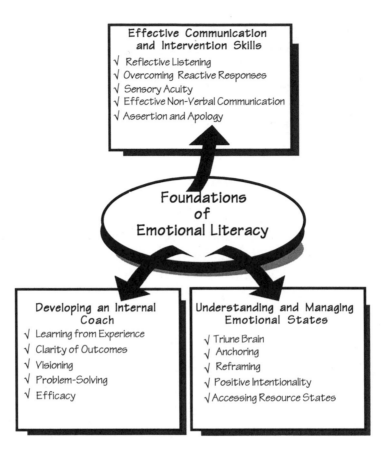

Figure 2.1.

on the three broad areas of competency (see Figure 2.1). The first competency incorporates work on *understanding and managing emotion in self and others.* This competency includes explanations and examples of the origin of emotion and the choices we have for recognizing and dealing with the physiological effects, as well as the emotional responses, in ourselves and others. The second competency addresses *effective communication and rapport building skills.* It outlines models for good listening out of conscious rapport-building skills, and strategies for using these skills in building relationships. The third competency area concentrates on *developing the internal coach.* The definition of self-coaching, skills and techniques for implementing a self coaching plan, and information on the role that Attribution Theory plays in developing a self coach are included.

Summary

Researchers such as Goleman (1995), Gardner (1983), Salovey (as quoted in Goleman, 1995), and Costa (1991) have identified characteristics of highly functioning people. Among those characteristics are the interpersonal and intrapersonal skills: the ability to listen with empathy, to monitor emotion in oneself and others, and to consciously choose our behaviors. Developing a constellation of skills such as these leads to emotional literacy, the possession of a repertoire of choices and strategies to support the individual's emotional interactions and decisions. People with emotional literacy are more successful at work, happier in general, and enjoy a sense of efficacy about managing their own lives.

These skills and strategies can be modeled and reinforced by adults, integrated into classrooms, and made the norm at school meetings and functions. Because emotional literacy is developable, it is an important area of intervention all of us in education need to address.

3

Understanding the Triune Brain

Contents

- Relationships Between Physiology and Emotion
- Examination of Evolutionary Model of Brain Development
- Explanation of Specific Primitive Survival Strategies
- Introduction of Higher Order Compensating Strategies

The sciences do not try to explain, they hardly even try to interpret, they mainly make models.

—John Von Neumann

What do all these phenomena have in common: road rage, the high-alert sensory awareness when we awaken startled in the middle of the night by a sound we fear might be an intruder, and the jumping to the worst-case scenario if we get a note from the boss asking us to report to his or her office to discuss our recent work? When we look at each of these situations, there is a pattern. It is a pattern of stimulus and response that has been with us and helped us to survive since the cave days.

So we get the note from the boss, and what is the first thing we think? Is it, "Oh, this is great. I'll have a chance to tell her about all the good things that are happening around here"? Probably not. In fact, our first response is likely to be much more visceral, much more physical, and much more instinctual. We are likely to wonder what went wrong and to begin looking for signs of impending disaster. Our brains immediately respond as if there is an unseen possibility of danger or threat. From an evolutionary perspective, this immediate, instinctual response is a useful survival mechanism because it helps us to anticipate and respond to danger. After all, a danger anticipated is one less likely to hurt us.

Our brains respond reactively whenever we perceive threat. In the middle of the night, we awaken to an unexpected sound. In seconds, we are fully conscious, our hearing seems unusually acute, our hearts pound, we are on what Goleman (1995) calls "high alert." All of our senses are tuned to the possibility of an intruder, a trespasser, or a danger. Again, the

> Worry is the cognitive anticipation of an negative outcome.
>
> Anxiety is the feeling we have when we worry.
>
> Stress refers to the physiological responses we have to perceived threat or danger.

FACTOID One of the first to write about this evolutionary approach to understanding human behavior was Carl Sagan (1934) in the book, *Dragons of Eden.*

FACTOID Firefighters and the police spend many hours training to overcome their "high-alert responses." Through practice, everyone can learn to manage their emotional responses.

brain is performing its evolutionary function—by sharpening our senses, we are more likely to foresee an enemy or an animal or situation that could turn against us. As an evolutionary adaptation, this mechanism provided heightened sensory awareness as we made our way through the forest, or tundra, or jungle.

The term *fight-or-flight* refers to the behaviors we manifest as a result of *high-stress response*. In some situations, we run away or disconnect from the stimulus, and we demonstrate passive or submissive behaviors. At other times, the behavior is more aggressive.

Today, that same neurophysiological response triggers heightened awareness whenever we perceive danger, threat, or trespass.

In some ways, this also explains road rage. The gut-level, visceral reaction to the person who cuts us off or who endangers our safety is another manifestation of this primitive brain taking over. The physical responses that we are conscious of—tensing of muscles in the face, arms, and stomach; the desire to violently exhale or yell; the clenching of teeth—all these are merely the aftermath of hundreds, if not thousands, of neurophysiological responses that occur largely out of the consciousness of most people. In addition to these observable physiological responses, there are other emotional reactions. When these are out of control, then rage, violence, and what some call "emotional hijacking" are not far behind.

In all three of these cases and in literally thousands more, the common link is the brain. There is one specific model of the brain that accounts for fight-or-flight behavior, instinctual instead of thoughtful problem solving, and for the often unfortunate results of the inability to manage emotions successfully.

Understanding this model of the brain is the first step toward greater emotional literacy.

In the next section, we will examine this model of the brain and relate it to the kinds of common situations we all face day to day. Next, we will investigate five strategies or techniques for managing one's emotions. Understanding these strategies will then lead to skill for helping others manage their emotions, as well.

The Triune Brain

Dr. Paul MacLean (1990), neurologist and former head of the National Institute for Mental Health, in a book titled *The Triune Brain and Evolution*, proposes a way of thinking about the human brain that he calls the *triune brain model*. Essentially, MacLean conceptualizes the human brain as the result of three evolutionary stages or developments, each of which added distinct characteristics and abilities that in sum make up the workings of the human brain. Current research continues to add to our understanding of the complexity of the brain and the actual neurological mapping of emotion within the brain's physiological structures.

It is important to remember that this model, like all scientific models, is a metaphor to help us understand the complex functioning of the human brain (see Resource A for a more detailed, scientific description of current neurological models). As a means for grasping human behaviors, however, this model explores the implications of the insight that the *primary function of the brain is survival*. MacLean's (1990) model integrates human behaviors, as well as brain functions and structures in his three-part model.

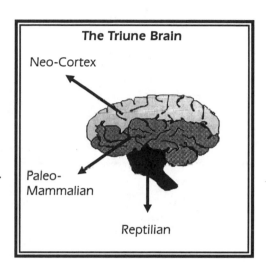

The Triune Brain

Neo-Cortex

Paleo-Mammalian

Reptilian

The Reptilian Brain

The oldest part of the brain, and the first to evolve, is referred to as the *reptilian brain*. Associated with autonomic systems and the hypothalamus, this part of the brain controls blood pressure, heart rate, hormone balance, the digestive system, and other involuntary systems throughout the body. It is this structure of the brain that keeps us operating even as our minds are occupied with other things. MacLean (1990) calls this the reptilian part of the brain because he theorizes

> MacLean's (1990) model is a kind of metaphor to help explain the complexity of the human brain. There are areas of the brain that correlate to the different functions that MacLean explains, but they are not isolated to specific levels.

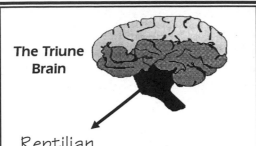

The Triune Brain

<u>Reptilian</u>
- Oldest, first evolved
- Instinctual
- Territorial
- Fight-or-flight response
- Autonomic systems

FACTOID When we are experiencing the reptilian response, all of the nonessential physiological systems temporarily shut down. Fingernail growth, hair growth, digestion all stop. The reason we get "cotton mouth" when we are under stress is that saliva production is actually a part of the digestive system. This also explains "butterflies" in the stomach.

that it evolved along with reptiles and that it correlates to the rudimentary brains of such animals. As such, the reptilian part of the brain also controls the same kinds of instinctual responses one expects from reptiles. For instance, mating rituals and the drives to reproduce, to find food, and to maintain and protect our territory are all instinctual, evolutionary response behaviors that help ensure the survival of a species. Territoriality, then, even in humans, is a reptilian behavior, and as MacLean (1990) suggests, our behaviors when our territory is threatened are first motivated by and characterized by primitive, instinctual responses.

In humans, this territoriality is evident in much of our day-to-day behavior. We choose to sit in the same spot in the same pew at church; at the dinner table, we sit in the same chair each night; at work, we try to park in the same parking place nearly every day, even when there are no assigned spots. And when someone else has taken our space, there is often a momentary twinge, a physical response that hearkens back to earlier evolutionary times. And this visceral response is not limited to just physical trespasses.

Whenever we perceive that a boundary has been crossed—whether it is physical, emotional, or psychological—there is the potential for a reptilian response. In some ways, this explains the crowd's strong visceral, physiological, and physical reactions to lost or gained yardage (territory) at a football game. Young children begin learning to manage this response as they "mark their territory" when they sit next to a brother or sister in the car or pew. In older children, the territory can be a favorite toy that becomes very difficult to share. In adolescence, a gang member's territory may be the few blocks of his or her neighborhood. Again, it is important to recognize that the perceived trespasses are not necessarily physical. When a person crosses the boundary of another's self-esteem, hard work, or even a project that the person feels he or she owns, the potential for a reptilian response is real.

The Paleomammalian Brain

The next oldest part of the brain, and the second to evolve, is referred to as the *paleomammalian brain*. MacLean (1990) conceptualizes this brain structure as a kind of appendage that evolved on top of the reptilian brain. Associated with the hippocampus and the thalamus, this newer ancient mammalian brain evolved along with the emergence of mammals, and it correlates to the brains and behavior of such animals. In addition to the ability to

FACTOID *Barry Rubeck, a Pennsylvania State University psychologist, studies what he calls "interim territoriality" (e.g., Rubeck & Carr, 1993). His research examines the way people behave in parking lots, at public telephones, and in library aisles. He has found that people talk much longer when someone else is waiting for the phone than when no one is waiting. In fact on average, the person stays on the phone 167% longer! How's that for territoriality! By the way, we stay in a parking space someone is waiting for, for approximately 7 to 12 seconds longer.*

function within a social hierarchy, this part of the brain is also correlated to curiosity, emotion, and the nurturing of young. In contrast to reptiles, mammals tend to live in social groups, and they display an underlying altruism. Emotion, nurturing, and curiosity are the bonds that hold the members of mammalian groups together and help these rudimentary communities survive and flourish. Many mammals ex-

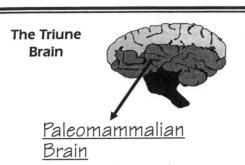

The Triune Brain

Paleomammalian Brain
- Second to evolve
- Curiosity
- Emotion
- Nurturing
- Altruism
- Social structures

plore and learn from experience; they work together to hunt, and they share the kill.

These kinds of behaviors are true of many animals. Elephants actually grieve when one of their herd dies. Mammals care for their young, sometimes for years. (In contrast, many reptiles will eat their young if they don't get away fast enough!) Bears and other mammals will examine a new, unfamiliar object introduced to their habitat. Gorillas and other great apes have been known to adopt and care for not only an orphaned offspring of another ape, but even of animals of other species. There are even cases of gorillas adopting and nurturing their own pet cats! Many people who work with dogs point out that truly effective training results from understanding the social needs and emotional development of these animals. Their work suggests that dogs see themselves as part of our "pack," and (if we are lucky) they see us as the head dog.

According to MacLean (1990), all of these behaviors are functions of the paleomammalian part of the brain. In mammals, as in humans, the paleomammalian exists in relation to the reptilian and works in conjunction with it. But unlike humans, mammals have only these two structures. It is the existence and development of the neocortex that distinguishes humans from all other animals.

The Neocortex

The *neocortex* is the newest part of the brain and the part that evolved and developed to its fullest in human beings. The kinds of functions and behaviors associated with this part of the brain are also the kinds of behavior that really define us. These include the ability to solve problems; forecast future consequences of present behavior; and to manipulate language, logic, and symbols. Essentially, all of our higher-order thinking skills, as well as our ability to be self-aware, are associated with this part of the brain. This "meta" function, our ability to think about our feelings as we feel them, provides us with the potential to understand and intervene in an otherwise instinctive, reactive response. The neocortex and its metacognitive ability allow us to learn from our experience to acquire ever more effective emotional tools and skills. It is this part of our brain that we use when we manage emotion and behavior in a literate way.

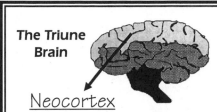

The Triune Brain

Neocortex
- Newest to evolve
- Higher-order thinking
- Language and symbols
- Logic
- Problem solving
- Predicting consequences
- Self-consciousness

Downshifting

Unfortunately, there are times when it becomes very difficult to access the functions of the neocortex. When we feel threatened or endangered, our brains *downshift*. That is, the reptilian cortex takes over the other parts of the brain in what Goleman (1995) calls an *emotional hijacking*. It is at this point that the reptilian, instinctual responses take command, and our neocortex becomes limited in its ability to manage.

This response has evolutionary benefit. When we lived in a hostile environment, when we needed instincts to survive, this response helped us respond quickly and effectively to threat. This explains why people who speak more than one language often revert to their first language when they are angry or feel threatened. During downshifting, much of the neural energy is expended by the reptilian brain; therefore, the brain falls back on the language that takes the least amount of cognitive effort. It also explains why, during an argument, we find it difficult to find the exact words we want; hours later, however, we can think through all of the things we could have said. Problem solving and logical reasoning are also difficult when we are afraid

Downshifting: Significant neural energy focused on fight-or-flight reptilian responses. This doesn't leave much room for carefully thought-out problem solving.

Anchoring is the skilled use of conditioned responses. We can teach ourselves to associate specific emotional behaviors to specific cues. It is one strategy that emotionally literate individuals use to intervene with themselves so that they can continue to have access to the neocortex, even under trying circumstances.

or highly anxious. In fact, all of our higher-order thinking abilities are compromised during downshifting.

Implications

The significance of these findings can not be overestimated. To many students, school is a highly competitive place where there are a limited number of points that can be earned, where learning is time driven, where they might be left behind, and where their grades will become public knowledge. Whether this is an accurate description is moot. If students perceive school this way, they are already in a state of high alert. Moreover, many young people (and adults) are unskilled at identifying the onset of downshifting, and they are equally unskilled at managing their emotions and behavior once it starts.

In each of the next chapters, I will identify, explain, and provide specific practice techniques for managing downshifting and emotion. These strategies are

- Anchoring
- Reframing
- Positive intentionality
- Accessing resource states
- Positive self-talk

Reframing is another cognitive strategy for remaining resourceful. It is the ability to manage the interpretations we make regarding events in our lives. It is the ability to create emotionally useful stories.

Accessing positive resource states is a coaching skill directed toward self or others. It refers to the ability to elicit appropriate emotional response.

In the next chapters, we will look at each of these skills in detail, and I will present specific strategies for developing them in ourselves and for teaching them to others.

Summary

In all circumstances, our brains are designed to first ensure our survival. Under perceived emotional or physical threat to our safety or sense of territory, that function of the brain overrides other cognitive functions, such as problem solving, logic, and higher-order thinking. Though this is a most valuable role of the brain, individuals who possess emotional literacy also develop skills and strategies to manage the tendency of our brains to revert to high-alert states and to the limited choices of fight or flight. There are several strategies that can be learned to aid in this endeavor, including anchoring, reframing, positive intentionality, accessing resource states, and positive self-talk.

4

Managing Emotions

Self-Awareness and Anchoring

Contents

- Definition of a resource state
- Explanation of anchoring
- Developing ability to consciously monitor emotion and physiology
- Strategies for accessing useful resource states

No one remains quite what he was when he recognizes himself.

—Thomas Mann

Robert Fulgum (1988) tells a story about giving crayons to some adult friends. He describes funny looks and laughter as these friends take the crayons and almost immediately begin to savor childhood recollections of the joys of a new box of crayons. Essentially, he is describing a *conditioned response.* Pavlov first uncovered this phenomenon in his now-classic experiment, and later, B.F. Skinner expanded on stimulus-response learning as the foundation for his theories of positive reinforcement (Gregory, 1987).

In much the same way, we respond, more or less unconsciously, to cues or stimuli throughout the day. The smell of crayons or the first notes of a popular song from our youth can trigger emotional and physiological responses that go largely unregulated for many people. Television advertisers, aware of this stimulus-response conditioning, work to create positive conditioned responses between their products and our emotions. Their basic strategy is to present images, songs, and spokespeople that we respond to in a positive way. The stronger the response, the better. Once this emotional response is established, the advertisers will then *anchor* their product to our emotional state. So, like Pavlov's bell, the product name triggers the physiological emotional response when we are in the store.

> Pavlov discovered that if each time he fed a dog he also rang a bell, in time, the dogs would respond physiologically to the bell as if it were the food itself. In other words, when he rang the bell, the animals were conditioned to salivate and have other physiological responses, even when there was no food present (Gregory, 1987). This is a conditioned response.

> Anchoring is the skilled use of conditioned response. We can teach ourselves to associate specific emotional behaviors to specific cues.

What the advertisers know is that we are usually not consciously aware that anchoring has occurred. So when someone like Michael Jordan, who engenders strong positive feelings in us, is linked to a particular product over and over, in time, the positive feelings we have toward the celebrity are transferred to the product. Likewise, coffee commercials that present sweet images of family and friends getting together and laughing and talking produce the kinds of warm, secure feelings that are then anchored to the product.

> **FACTOID** Many celebrity spokespersons have contracts that are contingent on their maintaining a positive public image.

The terms *emotional resource state* and *emotional state* refer to the combined physiological and emotional response to some stimuli, whether internal, external, or a combination. Thus, *mood* might be considered analogous to emotional resource state if we include the physiological as well as its affective and cognitive components.

Anchoring, however, is not solely the domain of advertisers. It is a completely natural human phenomenon that shapes our responses in myriad ways. Many of us have "comfort foods" that make us feel better when we are ill or blue. The foods that were anchored to feelings of safety and comfort in our youth trigger similar feelings years later. Most people have experienced meeting someone who reminds them of a person from their past. Often, that resemblance triggers an emotional response that has little to do with the here and now, yet it can

Reptilian Brain

The Triune Brain

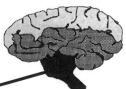

Stress is often a reptilian response, triggered by some external stimulus. The resulting physiological reactions actually reinforce the initial internal perception that we are in some danger. The reinforced perception then triggers an even stronger fight or flight response, which in turn leads to a deeper sense of anxiety, and the cycle becomes self-reinforcing, sometimes leading to behaviors that are counterproductive. Anchoring can break and or help us avoid this cycle.

profoundly affect our interactions with the person we've jut met. Smells, sounds, visual images, songs, people, almost any stimulus can become an anchor that triggers a response. Some of these responses are pleasant; some are not. In fact, much of our daily stress is the result of unmanaged reptilian responses triggered by some anchor. Again, these are just other examples of how the conditioned response influences not only our physiological and emotional states but our behaviors, as well.

Emotionally literate people recognize the power of these anchors and are conscious of their influences on us in everyday life. Instead of being unconsciously buffeted by these influences, these people have strategies for using anchoring to promote useful emotional resource states. And there are a number of specific strategies that can help all of us do this like experts.

FACTOID One strategy used by sports psychologists to help athletes such as divers, gymnasts, and skaters anchor useful resource states is to have them imagine they are some animal that has the attributes or characteristics that will support their reaching their goals. For instance, at a time when a skater or gymnast needs to be particularly graceful and strong in his or her movements, the athlete might picture himself or herself as an eagle soaring or as a leopard ready to spring.

There may be some value in rethinking the way we judge emotional resource states. "Good" and "bad," or even "positive" and "negative" may limit and predispose us to see some states as better than others and in some cases, to judge a particular emotional state as "wrong." These views distract us from what may be a more important question: "Is this particular resource state useful, right now?" Will this response state help me achieve my desired outcome?

Although there are still many half-truths and misconceptions regarding their specific strategies, stress management consultants and Olympic athletes were among the first to practice resource state management skills—that is, anchoring—to reach specific outcomes. One misconception even today in most stress management workshops is that the desired outcome is to reduce stress.

Although at first it may seem to be mere semantics, in reality, good stress management is really about learning how to create a resource state that is more useful than one where the individual's heart is racing and his or her blood pressure is skyrocketing. It is not that we are trying to *reduce stress;* instead, we are learning to determine what emotional state would be most appropriate in a given circumstance and then to create, or trigger, *that* state.

According to Harvard University researcher, Howard Gardner (1985), we each have at least eight different intelligences for expressing ourselves and for solving problems. Some of us rely on language, others on movement, still others use visual images or music. Because of these different ways of ways of experiencing, it may be useful, and powerful to experiment with multiple ways of translating and expressing our emotional responses. Journa-Journaling, drawing, sculpting, dance, collages, clay, songs, movement, color, visualizations, noise making, as well as talking and self-reflection may yield great insights.

Something to Try

Inventory talking is a learned strategy for developing greater sensory acuity and consciousness. Start by gathering a number of objects that you know are anchors for you. These could be mementos from your past—photos, particular foods, toys, or even songs. Next, sit quietly for a moment, and then one by one by one, allow yourself to fully experience the objects. After each one, write down (inventory) your recollections, images, emotions, and physical responses. Be careful to note not only your emotional responses but also the changes in your breathing, muscle tension, posture, and other aspects of your physiology.

Calmness, patience, or some other state may be the most useful at the moment. In fact, in some situations, the most useful resource state might very well be high alert or stress. But the two key questions remain, "What is the most useful emotional resource state for this situation, and how do I trigger that state right here, right now?"

After all, isn't this what athletes do? Or chess masters, or musicians, or firefighters, or Middle East peace negotiators? In each of these examples, the individuals must be able to trigger appropriate resource states for the task at hand. We talk about getting "pumped up," or "focused," or "in the groove," and in every case, the ability to create a useful emotional resource state is one of the factors that distinguishes the master from the novice.

And so it is with emotional literacy in life, with our loved ones, in times of peace and in times of chaos. And anchoring is a fundamental skill for consciously creating useful emotional states.

Learning to Anchor and Trigger Emotional Resource States

The first steps toward managing emotional resource states involve developing greater consciousness. It is important to recognize the physiological attributes that correlate to specific emotions. What is actually going on in our muscles, in our breathing, in our gestures and facial expressions when we are experiencing a particular emotion? What happens to our voice, its timbre and pitch, our rate of speech, and the volume of our sentences when we are feeling angry, or sad, or exhilarated? How tense are the muscles in our shoulders, chest, and arms when we are afraid or happy?

FACTOID One strategy taught in stress management workshops involves imagining a wonderful vacation spot (often the beach) where all the stresses, tensions, and anxieties melt away. The participants are encouraged to recall sights, sounds, and even the smells of this relaxing place. The emotional and physiological changes are remarkable. People relax—they use anchoring to create a resource state of relaxation. The same technique can be used to trigger any resource state. *Vividly recalling experiences from our past that contain the appropriate anchors can trigger any resource state.*

> **FACTOID**
>
> Try this: Ask students to list the ways they know they are hungry. Students will most likely list physical signals, such as "headache," "stomach growling," "light-headedness." As a beginning awareness activity, this exercise illustrates how often we ignore the signals our bodies send. After all, a person must regularly ignore many preliminary signals if pain, stomach sounds, or feeling faint are the ways he or she finally knows that he or she is hungry. In fact, some people will actually give a completely external signal—their clocks—as the signal they use. Many people are unaware of the physical feelings they experience.

Many people, children and adults alike, have been taught to ignore the sensations that signal a particular emotional response. Some people have difficulty distinguishing one emotion from another. Others have a very limited emotional palette; still others feel nothing at all, having learned to shut down their awareness of their sensations.

Of course, there are others who have a rich emotional life. They are able to discern subtle nuances in their own physiological responses. These are people with a broad spectrum of finely differentiated emotional hues. They are able to discriminate various shades of emotion and their specific physical sensations. It takes patience and practice to develop this kind of consciousness, and it is a necessary first step.

The next steps involve learning that anchors trigger-specific emotional responses. For instance, understanding that a particular place with its various sensory stimuli evokes a specific emotional state is the initial step in learning to recreate, or trigger, that emotional state at a later time. *It is of utmost importance to realize that those sensory details— those stimuli—are the anchors for the specific emotional resource state.* The effect of the vivid recollection of those sensory details makes anchoring possible.

Last, it is the ability to discern what emotional resource state is appropriate or useful in a given circumstance, as well as the possession of a wide range of anchored states, that leads to conscious choices and a rich emotional repertoire.

Activities and Strategies
for Teaching Anchoring

Each of the activities share at least two things: They all require reflection on the nature of emotion, and they all ask the student to record his or her observations regarding the physiology associated with that emotion. Essentially, we are asking students to be conscious observers of their own emotional experience and to record those observations. To be effective, students are encouraged to take a "time out" to process their experience in order to learn from that experience.

Over time, students can be encouraged to take more and more responsibility for monitoring their emotional responses and their concurrent physiological characteristics. One of the simplest approaches to this is journaling. There are many alternatives to the classic diary-style journal. As we look for ways to enhance emotional consciousness for all students, a variety of structured journal formats, as well as varied journaling subjects, may provide the greatest accommodation for the differences among individuals.

Traditional Diary-Style Journal

A classic, this can be the least structured of all. The student essentially reflects on his or her experiences, feelings, and reactions to events. Used for reactions to literature, current events, or life experiences, this kind of journal enables students to reflect on their emotional responses to a wide range of topics.

Another variation of the journal has students imagine themselves reacting from a number of different points of view—for example, as different characters in a story or from the perspective of members of different social, political, or historical groups.

It is important to remind students to make the connections between their reactions, their emotions, and the physical responses, as they are all interrelated.

Split-Entry Journal

Each page is divided in half by a vertical line. On the *right side* of the line, the student recounts an event, the plot of a story, a sequence of events, or a description of an interaction. The student can also be asked to perform specific academic assignments, such as solving story problems or taking notes from the text.

On the *left side*, the student describes his or her emotional responses, noting anchors and his or her own physiology.

Another type of journal, the *directed associative journal*, has a fancy-sounding name and can be the most highly structured.

The students are first given specific, short periods of time to brainstorm or "free write" single words or short phrases related to a series of directed topics. For instance, the teacher might say, "Take 60 seconds to write down as many words as you can that describe what you think and you feel about X."

After the first 60 seconds, the teacher instructs the students to "take another minute to list words that describe the physical sensations that go along with your feelings."

Last, the students are asked to circle the five to eight "most important" words from the lists and then to "weave

FACTOID

Many students have a phobic, or reptilian, response to certain kinds of academic tasks. Some students react to writing, art, sports, or math by downshifting. A split-entry journal can help students recognize their phobic responses. Students who recognize their reptilian responses and develop strategies for staying resourceful will do better on these tasks.

those words together in a paragraph." As part of their responses, the students explain how and why they decided to circle the words they chose.

The potential topics for this journal structure are limitless; almost any topic or assignment covered in class will have an emotional overlay. Almost all classroom discussion topics, any controversial subject, any topic or event from history could work. The seasons, holidays, visual images, sounds, TV shows, or commercials are also possibilities.

In addition to journaling, which is fundamentally a linguistic approach, we can use other strategies and other intelligences to become more emotionally literate. One of these strategies is called *charting the day*. In this approach, students create a graph of their emotions during a specific period of time or during a specific activity.

The goal is to uncover patterns of response and to identify the triggers of those responses. By charting responses and color coding them over a few hours, days, or weeks, students will gain insights about their own emotional lives. For example, the chart might be set up as follows:

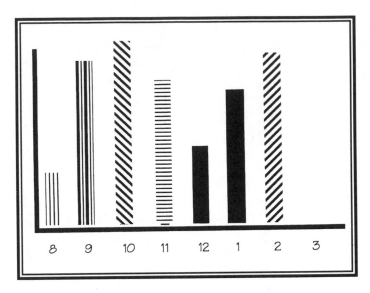

In this example, the strongest feelings occur at around 10 o'clock; the second strongest are at 9 o'clock. Once we begin to look more closely, we see that the emotions are pattern-coded. Perhaps the horizontally striped pattern represents worry or fear, and we see that at 9, there was strong anxiety over something. What could it be? If vertical stripes represent anger, then at 10 o'clock the diagonal strips would represent a combination of anger and fear.

At 11, we see just anger. The next steps, of course, would be to look at this pattern: anxiety leading to fear and anger followed by anger alone. What activities are occurring at these times of the day? What are the best outcomes in dealing with these concerns, and what strategies would be most useful and appropriate? These kinds of questions may be difficult to deal with at first, and so we (or the students themselves) may want to avoid them. These kinds of questions unasked, however, can leave the student unprepared to deal with life's difficulties.

Of course, the complexity of the charts, the number of patterns, and the duration covered by the charts can be adjusted to match the sophistication and developmental level of the individual student. Because of this strategy's strong visual elements, it is a powerful nonverbal

FACTOID An art teacher's daily assignment asks students to make a visual representation of their day using color and shape and line only (no symbols, words or "pictures" allowed). She finds that she must help students learn to be reflective and to understand their own feelings for them to make progress in this assignment; otherwise, she has found that the students draw the same thing every day.

way to uncover patterns of emotion. It is effective by itself or as a prewriting activity to help students see how they are feeling before they try to describe those feelings in writing. Colors can also be used instead of patterns.

Another strategy allows students to translate their feelings to a kinesthetic model. Here, we ask students to use clay, Playdoh, or even the popular foam modeling toys known as *Toobers and Zots again* to create sculptures of their emotions and feelings. Again, as a non-verbal expression of an emotional state, this strategy facilitates students getting a more clearly defined understanding of their emotions. The strategy can be closely structured or much more free form, depending again on the developmental level of the student. For some students, this approach will be especially powerful because it bypasses the linguistic filters that can block the full expression of feelings.

Last, for all students sometimes and for some students often, a verbal approach will be the most compelling. For these instances, we can use a two-partner verbal strategy that is called a *speak and feel exchange* (SAFE). In this strategy, students learn to verbalize their emotions and the physical sensations

FACTOID English teachers often find that students have more to say—either in writing or orally—when they have time and opportunity to understand their own responses to a story. These teachers explain their approach, saying, "How are students supposed to be able to respond to a story we are reading in a class if they aren't conscious of their own feelings first? If we don't teach them how to understand their own responses, they either search for some hidden meaning or else they just sit there waiting for me to tell them the right answer."

that accompany them. As a result, students can develop a deeper awareness of what they are feeling as well as an ability to articulate those sensations and emotions. This practice lays a strong foundation for the more complex conflict management and problem-solving skills that students will ultimately master. In fact, for students to be successful with many of the later strategies, they must have the ability to identify and articulate how and what they are feeling in real time.

In a SAFE, one student is the speaker and the other is the listener. As in the split-entry journals, the student must solve a social, interpersonal, or academic problem; the range of problem types is unlimited. Unlike the split-entry journal, this strategy requires that students be able to listen effectively. As the speaker thinks through the problem, the listener has four jobs. First, the listener is responsible for keeping the speaker talking. By demanding constant vocalization, the listener helps the speaker make the internal monologue explicit. The speaker's reflections, the connections between physiology and emotion, as well as leaps of logic and emotion, become more obvious to the speaker. This also helps uncover counterproductive self-talk and self-defeating beliefs.

The listener's second responsibility is to encourage the speaker to explore his or her own feelings and thoughts, without interruption. At the same time, the listener can help the speaker by periodically asking the speaker to pause and summarize what he or she has said. This kind of reflecting on a reflection is another example of a processing time out. The purpose here is to have the speakers hear themselves describe the progression of their thoughts, perceptions, and emotions and to look for patterns. Some of the uncovered patterns may be useful, productive, and highly beneficial; some may be dysfunctional. In either case, the listener's third responsibility is to encourage the speaker to uncover new approaches and possible action plans for solving or resolving the problem.

The listener's fourth responsibility is then to encourage the speaker to identify his or her positive outcomes for the particular set of circumstances and to brainstorm and consider alternative perspectives and strategies for achieving those outcomes.

In all cases, but especially when dealing with highly emotional, personal reflections, the listener's role is never to judge, fix, or solve the problem for the speaker.

The ultimate goal in all of these activities is to provide the individual students with opportunities for capacity building and for the development of self-coaching skills. This goal can never be reached unless we have faith in the students, and we must demonstrate that trust by being attentive to and honoring their struggles to understand their own emotional landscapes.

Each of us must learn to recognize and honor the subtle ways our bodies respond to emotional anchors and triggers. It is absolutely necessary for our students to acknowledge what they feel when they feel it if they are ever going to be able to become truly emotionally literate.

Summary

Our emotional lives are inundated with conditioned responses, sometimes prompted by people who can profit from our natural reactions to anchors, links we make between a product and an automatic physiological and emotional response. We can sharpen our abilities to access these responses ourselves by first becoming conscious of which anchors result in which responses. Then we are able to learn to revitalize the anchor and, as a result, to reframe the response to create a useful resource state.

This chapter introduces activities to help students begin to recognize the anchors and physiological responses in their day-to-day lives.

5

Communicating Through Reframing and Positive Intentionality

Contents

- Definition of reframing
- How ambiguity and context affect emotional responses
- Recognizing positive intentionality
- The reframing from position to interest

The real voyage of discovery consists not in seeking new lands but in seeing with new eyes.

—Marcel Proust

In the last chapter, we explored activities for helping students (and ourselves) become more emotionally aware, conscious of the triggers and anchors that affect our emotional states. As a result of this greater awareness, we can begin to manage these triggers and anchors that influence our emotional responses. In this chapter, we will explore another strategy—*reframing*—for managing emotion in ourselves and also as a way of influencing the emotional states of others. Reframing differs from other techniques because it focuses on latter stages of emotional response instead of the initial trigger of the emotion. *Reframing is the ability to manage the interpretations we make regarding events of our lives. It is the ability to create emotionally useful stories as or while the incidents in our lives unfold.* In this chapter, we will examine the hows and whys of reframing.

One of the key insights about emotion (and about communication as well) is that our emotional responses are almost always a result of our interpretations of the events in our lives. In most cases, the context has a significant influence on the interpretations we make. In some cases, the relationship we have with the other person or the expectations we have about the circumstances influence us to have one interpretation; in others, the context leads us to other interpretations and thus to other emotional reactions.

For instance, the words, "You look nice today," coming from a friend who we believe cares about us, elicits a pleasant emotional response and most likely

FACTOID

The term reframing comes from the fact that a picture will appear differently to us, depending on the color of the frame it is in. If you put a green picture frame around a painting, different colors in the painting seem to stand out. Even though the painting itself is the same, with a different color frame, other colors in the painting are emphasized. Although the picture itself has not changed, key perceptions have.

FACTOID

Reptilian responses are characterized by distortions of perception. During those times of high alert, people tend to interpret even ambiguous events as threatening. The evolutionary benefit of this was to help protect us from potential dangers in the environment. After all, if there is an unusual sound in the darkness, we are more likely to survive if we interpret the sound as a danger signal and then respond as if it is.

We are constantly telling ourselves stories about the motives and intentions of others. We constantly create meaning, and those interpretations drive our thoughts, emotions, and even our physiology. Our interpretations are affected by the circumstances and context of the events or words. Sometimes, the very same words will have different meanings for us simply because of the circumstances we are in. For instance, someone could say something that we clearly understand as a joke, but the same words in a different context would be hurtful.

an appreciative remark. On the other hand, the very same words coming from a person we believe is sarcastic elicits a totally different interpretation, a different emotional response, and a different remark.

To complicate matters, humans have a tendency to interpret ambiguous situations as threatening. So anytime we face an uncertain circumstance, it is more likely that our interpretations in those contexts will be negative. This makes sense from an evolutionary perspective: If unsure, expect (and prepare to respond) to the worst-case scenario. Two of the factors, then, that contribute to fight-or-flight response are *context* and *ambiguity*.

A key to managing our emotional states is to understand the effects of our ability to interpret events in a useful way. The stories we tell ourselves affect our perceptions of context and can substitute meaning for ambiguity. Ultimately, these interpretations and stories are powerful tools for managing our emotional responses. Figure 5.1 illustrates this.

Reframing is a conscious intervention in the second phase shown, where we interpret (or reinterpret) the context, the words, or the event itself. It is here where the story we tell ourselves has a significant impact on our emotions.

Not long ago, we were explaining this in a workshop when a woman raised her hand to recount an event from just a few days earlier. She was in an electronics store trying to determine which scanner would be best for her needs and budget. As she asked a salesperson for help, she was frustrated by his lack of attention and his short one- or two-word answers. She found herself getting angrier and angrier as she thought to herself, "How rude he is." "He has no right to treat me this way." "I'm trying to buy something, and he just doesn't care."

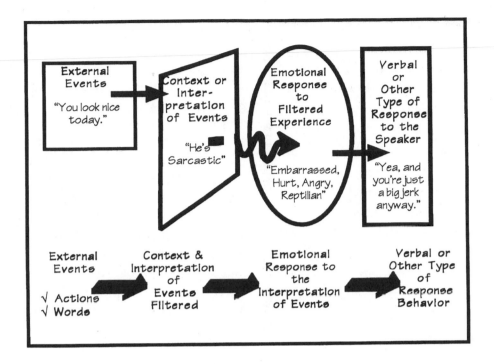

Figure 5.1.

Finally, she had just about had enough and said, "You don't seem to care very much about trying to help me!" With that, the young man broke into tears and said that he was sorry, that he had just gotten a phone call from his girlfriend who was leaving that morning to go to college. He was going to miss her, and he was heartbroken.

In a moment, the scenario changed for the woman; now, instead of being angry, she was sympathetic. She was telling herself a new story and therefore felt differently. The reframing of the young man's behavior elicited a different emotion. The anger was gone, replaced by a different response. Someone in the workshop asked the woman what she did next. She said, "My son went through the same thing, and he reminded me of him, and so the next morning I brought him homemade cookies"—a different response indeed to the one that may have resulted if the same behavior had not been reframed.

Everyone in the workshop laughed, of course, but the woman's actions point to the power of reframing. Just like a different color of picture frame can emphasize certain colors and thus elicit a different

One of the characteristics of those people with high emotional literacy is that they have a kind of internal coach that can reflect on what is happening in the moment instead of getting caught up and carried away. These people also understand that they are the only ones responsible for their feelings and actions. The person with high emotional literacy knows that he or she can control only himself or herself and that to try to do otherwise can lead to trouble. Reframing is a self-coaching tool to help us control our own responses.

response to a painting, so too, a different frame around an experience can bring out different emotions.

Sometimes, the power of this technique causes people to worry that we might "just be rationalizing and excusing inappropriate behavior." But this concern misses the point of reframing. The focus of this technique is ourselves, not the other person or even their behavior, for that matter. Using reframing effectively is a way to *manage our own emotions* so that we can make wise, deliberate choices about how we will respond. Otherwise, there is a good chance that we will respond reactively with some reptilian behavior. And although we can use reframing positively or negatively, the truth is that there is really no way not to frame an experience one way or the other. The question is, "Will this frame be useful or not? And then, "Should I reframe?"

In fact, reframing is one of those gifts that we cannot avoid and that keeps on giving. And once a person understands reframing, then he or she knows that when we worry, we are reframing; when we tell ourselves that there was a reason for something happening, we are reframing. Or when we stay angry for hours because someone did or said something and we give any meaning or reasons for it, we are reframing.

And yes, reframing is a kind of rationalization, but *this does not mean that we use reframing to excuse inappropriate behavior.* By maintaining our own emotional centers, we are in a better position to respond in the most useful, appropriate way. When it comes to choosing a course of action, it is often wise to be able to understand and control ourselves first, then to determine how we might respond to the behavior of others.

One of the first approaches to reframing is outlined in the work of those researchers who study resiliency. Waters and Lawrence (1993) describe their approach as a moving toward the healthy intentions that underlie dysfunctional behavior patterns. They see the dysfunction as a symptom not of some pathology to move away from but as of evidence of a limited repertoire of healthy options for achieving what very well may be a positive goal. They introduce the concept of *positive, or healthy, intentionality* as a reframing technique.

Essentially, to understand positive intentionality is to understand that almost all human behavior is motivated by individuals' attempt to protect themselves and to thrive in some way. Obviously, this does not mean that all behavior is positive nor does it mean that we should accept all behavior. And of course, there should be consequences for behaviors that are hurtful, selfish, or violent.

What positive intentionality does suggest, however, is that *inappropriate behaviors may be the best or perhaps the only ones a person has for meeting a goal*. For instance, many students have learned strategies for seeking attention that ultimately get them into trouble. The behavior, whether it is acting out, shutting down, or joining a gang, is a strategy for being noticed. The goal, getting attention, is positive; the problem is the limited repertoire of strategies for reaching the goal.

Unfortunately, many young people today have very limited approaches for reaching what could be a positive goal. As an example, we could look at the positive intention of having control and predictability in one's life. Predictability and a certain degree of control are good things; in fact, they support efficacy and self-esteem. Many children (and adults) are desperate to have some sense of predictability and control in their lives. Sadly for some, the only way they have for creating this sense of control is through anorexia or bulimia. For others, their sense of control is found through bullying others. In adults, we sometimes see that this desire for control is gained by intimidating their spouses.

What then do eating disorders, bullying, intimidating, and joining street gangs have to do with positive intentionality? Sadly, it is this: These are the best (and perhaps the only) alternatives some people have. They are doing the best they can with what they know, with the life experiences they've had, and with the skills and alternatives at their disposal. Feeling empowered, belonging to a team, and knowing that you fit in are all wonderful, positive intentions. Unfortunately, if no one ever took the time to teach you to play an instrument, to catch a ball, or to play with others in a play group, then it may appear to you that your only alternative is to join a gang of other kids just like you, kids with poor emotional skills, who lack empathy, and who have difficulty in their relationships.

Reframing Strategies

Each of the following activities have at least two things in common. First, they all explore our ability to reframe experience and thus to come to realize that our first reaction to a particular event is often a response to our hallucination of what that event means. Second, each of these activities provides students with opportunities to develop empathy for others.

Red Light, Green Light is an approach for reframing. It is a way for students to learn to accept their feelings. In this technique, the *red light* applies to anything that is upsetting. So if one student is refusing to share or is provoking some conflict, the student who has learned this strategy will first recognize his or her feelings and identify them, as well as identifying the behavior that is upsetting. Once the behavior and emotion (the red light) are identified, the student moves on to the *yellow-light question.*

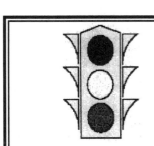

A *red-light behavior* is something someone else does that makes you see red.

The yellow-light question is used to help the student do two things. First, it helps the student see and understand the motives, context, and perspective of the other person. Second, it provides a way for the student to generate useful options for dealing with the troubling situation.

The yellow-light question is, "Under what circumstances or conditions would I behave like that?" Here, the student is encouraged to brainstorm many options. It is important to help the student realize that although the

The *yellow-light question:* Under what circumstances or conditions would I behave like that?

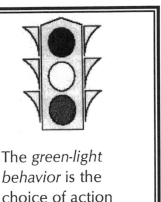

The *green-light behavior* is the choice of action that you take as a result of reframing.

first response might be to say that he or she would *never* respond that way, there *must* be some circumstances that would lead him or her to such behaviors. It is his or her responsibility as an emotionally literate person to imagine what they might be. Using this strategy, students will begin to recognize that sometimes it is lack of knowledge, skill, or information that contributes to inappropriate behaviors or decisions. Emotionally literate people take this into consideration as they choose their own courses of action. After the student has completed answering the yellow-light question, it is time to decide how to "go."

The *green-light* step is where the student chooses a specific behavior, choice, or decision—a way to go forward. With his or her understanding of possible root causes or contributing factors that have led to the other student's inappropriate behavior, the emotionally literate student can make better choices regarding his or her own response. This is the green-light choice. By this time, the student is much more likely to be able to make a clearer, wiser decision.

There are a number of classroom applications of Red Light, Green Light. Students can use this to explore points of view and behaviors of individuals and groups in current events or historical contexts. Students can use this to imagine the intentions of characters who make either wise or unwise decisions and choices in stories. It even can be used to discuss author intent and theme. For instance, the question, "Under what circumstances would you write a story or poem like this one?" can help the students see authors as real people who are working to understand and communicate some things about life just as they are. The ultimate goal is for students to use this strategy with their family, friends, team mates, and peers. During team and class meetings, when there are conflicts or misunderstandings and hurt feelings, Red Light, Green Light could be applied.

Another strategy is found in the work of William Ury (1991a, 1991b) and Peter Senge (1994), as well as others who work with people searching for so-called win-win solutions to difficult problems, and it is called *interest-based negotiation*. This is another type of reframing technique.

To teach this strategy, the teacher must first understand some distinctions between *positions* in a dispute and underlying *interests*. As we look at these two concepts, there are some important distinctions between them, and understanding these differences often helps uncover win-win solutions.

First, a *position* is often the initial stand that people take when they are in a dispute or conflict. The position represents what the person wants. Usually, the positions in the dispute are mutually exclusive. For instance, if I want the car at 7:00 o'clock, and my spouse wants the car at the same time, the car can't be in two places at once. Moreover, when participants in a conflict are defending their positions, there is very little flexibility, and the outcome is usually some form of win-lose result. (Only one of us will have the car and the other person loses.) Because the result is win-lose, the conflict is often settled as a result of which party has more power, control, or influence. These characteristics of *positional negotiation* make this approach a less useful and less flexible approach than an interest-based approach.

Flexibility and collaborative negotiation are the hallmarks of the interest-based approach. *Interests* represent the underlying motivation that drives a person's position. Almost always, interests can be mutually inclusive, allowing win-win solutions. Over time, this approach builds trust and a collaborative foundation for teamwork, relationship building, and cooperation. To make the shift from position to interest, the emotionally literate person must first do three things:

1. Manage emotions
2. Provide a structure for uncovering both parties' interests
3. Provide a structure for collaborative problem solving to find a win-win outcome

Earlier, we explored strategies for understanding and managing emotion. These same strategies, applied during this kind of negotiation, are important in order to maintain a cognitive, deliberate, and wise approach.

From this cognitive approach, the participants must use some structure to uncover their interests. There are two simple questions that can do this. One such question is, "What would having [whatever the position is] do for you?" The alternative question is, " What would having [whatever the position] bring you?"

It is important to note two things here:

1. Emotion management is vital so that both people in the nego-tiation are safe from reptilian responses.
2. Both questions avoid asking the other person why he or she wants what he or she wants. *Asking "why" elicits a rationale for the position;* instead, the emotionally literate person is trying to uncover what drives the position.

Often, a very skilled person might combine these two points by saying something like, "Let's suppose you get X; let's just imagine that for a moment. Help me understand, what would having that bring you?" Once both parties answer this kind of question, they are ready to begin collaborative problem solving.

As an example, we can continue with the car dispute. If the posi-tions are, "I want the car at 7 o'clock" versus "No, *I* want the car at 7:00," then the questions might sound like this:

Rob: Let's suppose you had the car at 7:00; what would having the car then do for you?

Kathy: I would be able to see Donna. She's only in town tonight, and we want to get together.

Rob: Okay, and if I had the car at 7:00, I would be able to get to a meeting with a client that I have to be to on time.

At this point, the interests are clear. Kathy wants to see her friend, and Rob wants to get to a meeting. The next step is to formulate a problem statement.

The statement structure we recommend always starts with the same two words: "How to," followed by the interests connected by the word "and." In this case, it would be, "*How to* have Rob get to his meeting on time *and* have Kathy get to see Donna?"

This problem statement has lots of solutions. One of us could drop the other off, we could arrange other transportation, Donna could come over for dinner, Rob could have the meeting near the place where Kathy and Donna will have dinner. What is important is that

The *how-to statement is a powerful tool* for unlocking the creative, problem-solving parts of our minds. If we are going to spend time, effort, and resources to solve a problem, it makes sense to define the problem well. A how-to statement is one way to do this. By beginning our statement with the words "how to," we invite the mind to begin generating solutions almost immediately.

Try this:

Tell a friend that you are about to ask her a question. Ask your friend to carefully track her thinking as you ask her the question to see if she can avoid imagining an answer. Then ask her this question, "I am wondering if you can imagine how to have snow in New York City in July?"

You'll probably find that as soon as a person hears a question that begins with these magic words, his or her mind immediately begins to generate answers, even when the person doesn't mean to.

(a) there is much greater flexibility and creativity in the solutions, (b) the solution is win-win (both parties can have their interests met), and (c) the parties have avoided the negative emotion that often accompanies positional negotiations.

The three-step graphic presents a chart of the steps for moving from position to interest.

These steps can be applied in almost all cases. If the positions of the parties are rooted in some tangible object, like having the car, these steps are clear and obvious. When the interests are more symbolic or emotional, the same steps apply, although it may require more practice in emotion management to do so. For instance, if the interest behind having the car is, "It will let me know that I'm really important to you," then more emotional literacy is probably necessary. It is easy to balk at what might feel like emotional blackmail.

The person with great emotional literacy is more likely to see this emotional interest as simply another interest, and the how-to statement would reflect the reality of the two interests: "How to have Kathy see Donna and have Rob know that Kathy thinks he is important?" In many situations, these emotional or symbolic interests are actually the most important. To understand this creates greater and greater opportunities for teamwork and relationships that are strong, open, and emotionally sound. Without this structure, Rob might get the car (his posi-

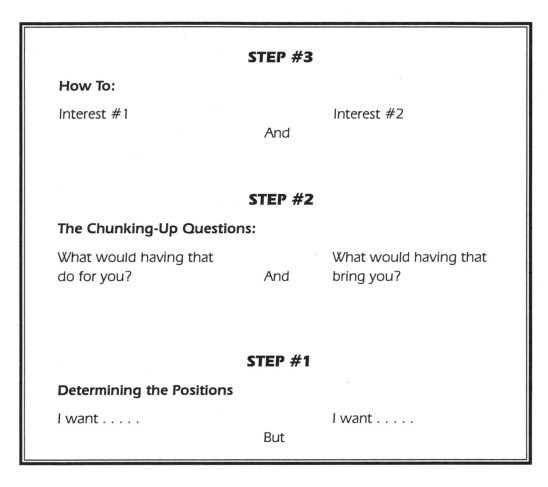

Figure 5.2.

tion), but he might get it anchored to such negative feelings that the interest is subverted. He could end up getting the opposite of what he actually wants. Unfortunately for many, this happens much too often, and being unskilled makes managing relationships difficult.

Fortunately, we can help students and ourselves develop new approaches to understanding and dealing with family, friends, and, in fact, all relationships. Developing true empathy is one aspect of this kind of emotional literacy. The importance of understanding other people's motivations or intentions *empathically* is different from the kind of "meaning making" that often occurs. Empathic understanding embraces the other person's reality; we see and feel, at least to some extent, the context, frame of reference, and the reality that the other person experiences. On the other hand, instead of empathic understanding, we might rationalize our negative emotional response to someone else's behavior. This rationalization can attribute motives and intentions that justify our response; it can actually interfere with empathy.

Summary

The human brain makes sense of the universe by constantly telling itself stories about what it experiences. It is the way we make meaning out of chaos; the story gives us a frame from which to operate and respond. Highly emotionally literate people learn to reframe or retell the story of some experiences as a way to manage their emotions and behaviors.

Recognizing *positive intentionality* and learning to negotiate from position to interest are two key strategies that enable a person to reframe, to tell themselves a more useful story.

6

Reflective Listening and Overcoming Reactive Responses

Contents

- Understanding the power of perceptual filters
- Exploration of the listening cycle
- The steps for rigorous, reflective listening
- Overcoming reactive responses
- Gender-related characteristics of human communication

When we listen to people there is an alternating current, and this recharges us so that we never get tired of each other.

Brenda Ueland

Communication, communication, communication—it seems as if every day, there is more demand for good communication. At home, at work, with friends—in fact, in every aspect of our lives—the ability to understand and be understood, the ability to make connections with others, and the ability to avoid and or manage conflicts is basic to making our relationships work. But as much as we try to understand each other, as hard as we try to get past the filters and distortions in everyday

Mental models are deeply ingrained cognitive maps that shape our understanding of the world. These models include our assumptions, generalizations, expectations, and theories of how the world is structured. These mental models influence our perceptions. Albert Einstein put it this way: "Our theories determine what we measure." Mental models even influence what we pay attention to.

Reflective listening is a four-step communication cycle, where the listener observes and takes in verbal and nonverbal cues from the speaker; then the listener processes those cues and forms a hypothesis about what the speaker is thinking and feeling. Last, the listener tests this understanding. The cycle continues as the listener attends to additional cues.

interactions, the truth is—it's not that easy. It takes rigor and self-discipline to overcome our deeply held mental models and to really listen. Well-honed communication skills are developed only as the result of conscious effort and choice. These skills are fundamental to emotional literacy, and in this section, we explore some communication essentials.

Specifically, we will examine the difference between *reflective listening* and *everyday listening*. We will learn and apply elements of nonverbal communication to build rapport, and we will focus on two other communication templates: *assertion* and *apology*.

Listening: The Foundation Communication Skill

Obviously, good communication is a two-way street. We all need to be able to clearly express our thoughts, ideas, and emotions. In addition, we need to be able to take in and understand the words, thoughts, and feelings of others. *Good communication is a cycle of expression and interpretation.* One person expresses his or her perceptions, the other person tries to comprehend, and then (as they do in every true conversation), the roles reverse.

During this process, there are subtle signals being sent back and forth. Some of the signals are the words themselves; some are nonverbal cues, such as tone of voice, gesture, and facial expression. Some of the signals are directly related to the content of the communication itself —the thoughts, ideas, events, and perceptions that are being communicated. Some of the cues reflect the emotional states of both the speaker and the listener. Many people think that good communicators focus on the skills of expression; that is, they think the best communicators are most concerned about being clear,

Assertion and apology are two communication templates for handling the difficult times when someone has trespassed over some boundary. They help protect both the relationship and the boundaries.

precise, and powerful in their expression of their points of view. After all, it certainly seems as if the speaking part of the communication process is the only *active* side. The listening side of the cycle seems passive; it seems like it takes little effort to hear someone. That comes naturally. Right?

Wrong. Most people think they are good listeners; unfortunately, the opposite is true. Good listening is a skill that takes great rigor and self-control. Good listening is actually the hallmark of the best communicators and also of those people with high emotional literacy. It involves a presence of mind, the ability to attend to hundreds of verbal and nonverbal cues, to recognize and track ongoing feedback. It requires conscious cognitive processing of the stream of information that passes between people when they talk together. The emotionally literate listener recognizes that his or her beliefs, emotions, and assumptions can filter and distort what the

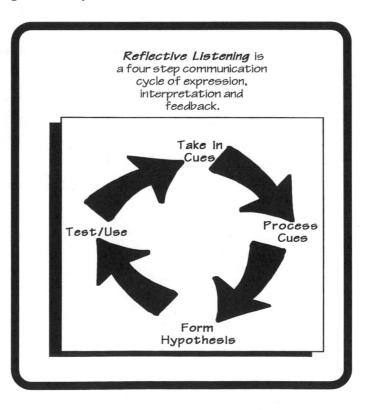

Reflective Listening is a four step communication cycle of expression, interpretation and feedback.

Take In Cues

Process Cues

Form Hypothesis

Test/Use

> *Rapport* is a short-term psychological state in which people feel that the lines of communication are wide open. At a time of deep rapport, the people involved have nearly all of their conscious thought processes focused on what they have to say, instead of on aspects of the relationship. They often will feel safe, comfortable, secure, and accepted.

other person is saying. Good listening takes great discipline and self-control; it is an active, conscious, humbling process of managing ourselves. Without humility, it is very difficult, if not impossible, to create even the opportunity for good communication to take place.

Basic Distinctions

There are many kinds of listening, and each kind requires specific kinds of cognitive and emotional skills. Debative, argumentative listening requires an emotional and cognitive stance that is very different from the stance associated with the listening we do when we want to learn something new or when we hear a story. Likewise, there are differences between *everyday listening* and *reflective listening*.

> *Everyday listening* is a three-step communication process. The listener takes in the cues, then processes those cues, and finally forms a hypothesis. This kind of listening is much less rigorous than reflective listening because the listener does not verify nor test his or her understanding.

Everyday listening is much less demanding and much more casual than reflective listening. Although everyday listening suffices much of the time, it is reflective listening that is the foundation of all the other communication skills. Without the ability to listen reflectively, a person striving for high emotional literacy is severely limited. Reflective listening is the underpinning of effective communication and a *must have* interpersonal skill.

> *Reflective listening is a key to emotional literacy. It is the foundation for avoiding conflict and for assertions. Good reflective listening is like the "Swiss army knife" of emotional literacy, and many people think they are already good listeners. What they don't know is that truly good listening demands rigor and self-control.*

Definition for Skillful Listening

Almost all forms of listening share at least the same first three steps in the process; reflective listening adds a fourth step that provides a way for the listener to verify his or her understanding of the speaker's meaning.

The first step involves observing the cues and signals that are part of the speaker's communication. The verbal cues obviously include the speaker's words and tone of voice. The use of certain metaphors, words that connote sadness or joy, and the actual recounting of the events or facts of a story are often the primary structural element of the communication. In addition, the rate, volume, and emotional timbre of the voice are also among the verbal cues that influence our understanding of the speaker's meaning. The verbal component also includes sighs, pauses, and other cues that affect the fluidity of the speaker's language. Hesitations, long pauses, trouble finding the words, as well as myriad other features of the speaker's verbal message affect us. And even though these influences are often outside of our conscious awareness, they nevertheless affect our perceptions and understanding of the speaker.

The second step is so immediate and we are so accustomed to doing it that most of the time, we don't even realize that we are doing anything at all. We screen, filter, and sift through the cues from Step 1. We analyze, prioritize, or in some other way organize the cues so that they begin to make sense for us in terms of our past experiences or expectations. Sometimes, we (unconsciously) distort the actual message so that it matches our expectations and experiences. And although this is a perfectly human thing to do, it does make communication difficult.

Step 3 is closely linked to Step 2. Once we have sorted, organized, and prioritized the speaker's signals, we next form a hypothesis—our best educated guess—about which signals are most important, what

> **FACTOID**
>
> When engineers design fax machines, they build in a fail-safe feature so that the machines can verify that the information was received correctly. Before a receiving machine prints the fax, it sends everything it received back to the original machine with a kind of electronic question mark attached, as if to ask "This is what I got. Is this what you sent?" The sending machine verifies and sends a big "yes." Then and only then will the other machine print the fax.

they mean. Last, we form our hypothesis about what it is that the speaker must really mean.

In the kind of casual chitchat that marks many conversations, these three steps are usually adequate. However, when it is important to make sure that the information is communicated accurately, we must move to reflective listening and its fourth step.

The purpose of the fourth step is to build in a feedback loop, a kind of fail-safe measure to verify that the listener received the speaker's message accurately. Computer engineers understand the need and the importance of having this kind of verification system in place whenever important information is to be transferred from one system to another. For instance, when a fax machine in Chicago sends a document to a second fax in Syracuse, the two machines go through a verification process. The first machine sends the data; the second machine temporarily stores the data before doing anything with it.

Every so often, the second machine will send the data it has received back to the first machine with a question mark attached. In effect it asks, "This is what I received. Does it match what you sent?" If the answer is "yes," then (and only then) the machine will actually print the data. The reason engineers build in this feedback loop is simple: They know that sometimes there is static on the line, that sometimes there will be some kind of interference, and so they build in a protocol so that the receiving fax machine doesn't print garbled, distorted text.

Just as the server at the fast-food drive-through window repeats your order, a good reflective listener will verify his or her understanding before jumping in.

So the listening process involves taking in the cues, processing those cues, forming a hypothesis, and then in the fourth step, reflective listening goes further, verifying the hypothesis by testing it with the speaker. Because all human communications have some emotional overlay, the listener reflects not just the content but also his or her understanding of the speaker's emotional stance, as well. The following examples illustrate that reflections can take many forms:

"You are feeling sad that your friend is moving."

"You're excited about your new team."

"When you think of all the work that's still left on the project, you get worried."

"Because of the time, you're determined to find a better way to complete the work."

"You feel Bill's answer is wrong because he forgot to use the order of operations."

"You're a little confused because you think the answer should be three, not two."

It is worth noting again that each of these examples communicates that the listener understands the speaker on two levels:

1. The topic (whether it is a friend moving, the amount of work, or even an answer to a classroom math problem)
2. The emotion, feeling, and attitudes of the speaker (sadness, excitement, determination or confusion)

And although the syntax of these reflections can take many forms, there is at least one structure that should probably be avoided. In our work with literally thousands of people, we have found that many people are put off by the words, "So I think I hear you saying that . . ." For them, this preamble makes the listener's honest attempt sound artificial, stilted, or contrived, at best, and at worst, dishonest or manipulative. Because many people are sensitive to these kinds of beginnings, teachers may want to consider teaching students to avoid them.

The easiest way to avoid these preludes is simply to begin with whatever words would come after the word "that" in the preamble. Instead of "I hear you saying that you're happy about the grade," the listener can say, " You're happy about the grade." The same goes for

FACTOID Down-shifting is a main cause of many difficulties in communication. Once on high alert, we begin to interpret words, actions, and events as potentially threatening. It is one of the reasons why change is so difficult.

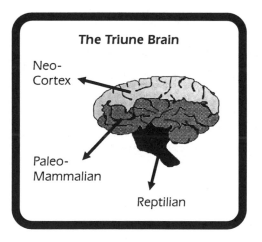

The Triune Brain

Neo-Cortex

Paleo-Mammalian

Reptilian

"I think I hear you saying that . . . ," "You must be feeling that . . . ," or any of the other introductions that someone might make. In this case, simpler is better.

In the best of all worlds, once around the listening cycle, both the speaker and the listener could be sure they had communicated clearly. Unfortunately, in real life, it is usually necessary for the listener to travel around the cycle a number of times. Each time, the listener and the speaker are more able to create, refine, and ultimately reach a clearer understanding. It is a joint improvised creation of meaning that rests with both parties. Often, when there is skilled reflective listening, the speaker comes to a more subtle or complex understanding of his or her own thoughts. In any case, the skills of reflective listening offer a concrete means for cleaning up the communication, for gaining a wiser perspective, and for lowering negatively charged emotion.

Reactive Responses and Questions: Roadblocks to Good Reflective Listening

When someone begins to learn and practice reflective listening, a number of habits and reactions begin to interfere with the person's attempts to listen well. Two of these are reactive responses and asking questions that are not really questions.

A *reactive response* is a stimulus-response reaction to something the speaker says. Picture a person, having decided to practice good listening, sitting down with someone to try to truly understand the other person's perspective and point of view, but then the speaker says something that triggers an emotion in the listener. If, as a result of the emotion, the listener interrupts the speaker by judging, problem solving, or changing the subject, he or she has interfered with the communication process. And most likely, the speaker will simply shut down. This is the danger of reactive responses; they sabotage the listener's good intentions and can be the root of communication problems in general. They interfere with the speaker's ability to

> Downshifting
>
> Significant neural energy focused on fight or flight reptilian responses. It doesn't leave much room for carefully thought-out problem-solving.

express him or herself and also interfere with the listener's ability to reflectively listen.

> A *reactive response* is a stimulus-response reaction to something a speaker says. Once the listener reacts, the focus is taken off of the speaker. Essentially, reactive responses interfere with the speaker expressing him- or herself. As soon as we begin any of these reactive behaviors, we have stopped listening and we begin doing something else.

> There are three categories of reactive responses:
> • Judging and blaming
> • Parenting and problem solving
> • Avoiding and diverting

It is important to note that reactive responses are not necessarily bad nor wrong. In fact, in some circumstances, specific kinds of reactive responses can be the most appropriate approaches to dealing with a problem or situation. There are many times when a specific kind of reactive response is absolutely necessary and useful.

But, and this is the key point, *as soon as we begin any of these reactive behaviors, we have stopped listening,* and we begin doing something else. And although there are a

Gender-Related Differences

All of us get caught in re-active responses from time to time. Most people tend to gravitate to some forms more than others. Deborah Tannen (1990), in *You Just Don't Understand*, points out that there are even gen-der-related differences in our language patterns. Women, she says, engage in *rapport-talk*; men engage in what she calls *report-talk*. These differences in style are even evident in the kinds of reactive responses we tend to use.

Because women tend to engage in *rapport-talk*, they often focus their talk around making connections and maintaining relation-ships. In a reactive mode, this might translate to a tendency toward soothing or reassuring.

The *report-talk* that men use is characterized by providing information and solving problems, and in a reactive mode, this can translate into fixing, asking questions, or offering solu-tions.

number of specific reactive behaviors, they can be organized into three general categories.

One of these categories refers to those behaviors that are *judgmental*. This category includes behaviors such as agreeing, disagreeing, criti-cizing, blaming, and praising. Certainly, there is nothing inherently wrong with agreeing or disagreeing nor with many of these behaviors per se, but each of these responses will take the focus off the speaker and thus interrupt the listening process.

Much of the time, these responses are actually in service to the lis-tener. It is as if the listener is made uneasy by something the speaker

Categories and Examples of Reactive Responses

Judging	1. Agreeing or disagreeing
	2. Criticizing or blaming
	3. Diagnosing
	4. Praising
Parenting and Solving	5. Ordering
	6. Threatening
	7. Moralizing
	8. Advising
	9. Questioning
	10. Problem solving
Avoiding	11. Logical Arguing
	12. Reassuring
	13. Diverting
	14. Understanding
	15. Joking

has said, perhaps triggering some unsettled feelings. If the listener typically deals with the ambivalence by quickly compartmentalizing or boxing the ambiguity away, then he or she is likely to do the same thing to the speaker. If the listener can't listen to him or herself, he or she probably can't listen to others. Interestingly, then, the ability to listen, to be in the presence of another's difficult or strong emotion, may in fact be a measure of a person's degree of self-awareness.

A second category of reactive responses describes the *parenting* or *fixing* behaviors. These often include advising, questioning, and problem solving. Here too, the reactive behavior interferes with the

FACTOID Robert Dilts (1990), Peter Senge (1990, 1994), and others have written extensively on the relationships between our beliefs, roles, and behaviors. They have found that *our perception of the role—the job we have to do and the beliefs we hold about it—has a significant impact on the choices, decisions, and skills we make and use.*

speaker. It is likely that when the speaker describes the presenting problem, it is merely the initial symptom or signal that the speaker is trying to figure something out. If being in the presence of the dilemma, difficulty, or circumstance is uncomfortable for the listener, she or he might try to make it go away by fixing it. If the listener can tell the speaker what to do, or make a suggestion, ask questions, or even demand that the speaker take one action or another, then the listener no longer has to tolerate the uncomfortable feelings.

Sometimes, the role of problem solver, parent, or rescuer is so ingrained that a person begins offering solutions and suggestions for fixing the problem even before the speaker has finished explaining what it is. Teachers, supervisors, principals, and parents often fall into using this category, and it is often because they believe that to do their job well, they must be able to solve the problems of those who depend on them.

The last category is *avoidance.* Joking, changing the subject, reassuring, diverting, and logical arguing fit here. When we remember that reactive responses are usually a way for the listener to protect him- or herself from having to actually experience some difficult emotion or circumstance, the behaviors in this category become obvious. So, for instance, the speaker is describing a painful conflict or perhaps the breakup of a romantic relationship. If the topic and its emotions are too close, or if the listener has no other way of managing his or her emotions, then that listener will probably do something to avoid actually talking about the feelings.

As Deborah Tannen (1990, 1994) points out, men and women have different tendencies for avoidance. If there are strong emotions, men will tend toward joking, logical arguing, or diverting. Changing the subject or making a joke allows the listener to simply move on linguistically. Logical arguing, on the other hand, may be an attempt to lower or even eliminate the high emotion by taking a linear, rational, or cognitive approach to the emotions. Although it may sound absurd, this is an approach that we actually teach young children when we say things like, "big boys don't cry," or "sticks and stones will break your bones, but names will never hurt you," or even, "don't let it bother you." And there are still many well-meaning people who say things like, "don't be a sissy." And although men are not the only ones who practice avoidance, obviously, these kinds of lessons learned early in life do more than simply make it difficult for men to listen; in some cases, it even makes it difficult to feel.

Women, too, practice avoidance but with different strategies. Women tend more toward reassurance and "understanding." For them, it is a matter of convincing the speaker that the situation is really not as bad as it seems and that everything is going to be just fine. Often, this may come in the form of assurances

> **FACTOID**
>
> Deborah Tannen (1990, 1994, 1998) is a professor of linguistics at Georgetown University. The author of numerous scholarly articles, she studies the way language is used by specific groups within different contexts. She has identified gender-related differences in language, as well as the dynamics of communication in the workplace. Her latest book is *The Argument Culture*.

that the speaker is not alone, that he or she is not the only one who has faced such difficulties, and that others have survived. For instance, a listener caught in this kind of response might say something like, "Oh, the same thing happened to my sister; she had a terrible time at first. But you know everything worked out. She felt . . ." Of course, this takes the focus off the speaker, and it also interferes with the speaker even experiencing his or her emotions. It saves the listener from having to actually deal with the here and now.

Sometimes, the "understanding" response serves the same purpose. When someone is expressing some difficult emotion or point of view, the understanding response will shut him or her down: "Oh yes, I understand, uh huh, I understand completely, the same thing happened to me." What is unstated but understood in this response is the

FACTOID

Most questions aren't really questions at all. In fact, there are some linguists who suggest that in some contexts, up to 90% of those sentences that end with a question mark are either requests for action, judgments, or statements of opinion disguised as questions. After all, this kind of social convention is so well understood that if someone asked if you have a watch, and you simply said, "Yes," they would think you were making a joke!

parenthetical, "So you don't have to say anything more; we don't have to keep talking about this because *I understand completely, even before you finish telling me.*"

Another roadblock to good listening and to building trust are questions that are not really questions at all. In fact, most questions that we ask may not be real questions. Often, questions are judgments, requests, or statements that are disguised as questions, often with poor if not disastrous results. For instance, when a colleague asks, "Don't you think it is getting close to a time for a break?" it is obvious that he or she is probably doing more than just wondering about your position on the lunch issue. In fact, the person is communicating an opinion about taking a break. When someone in a cooperative group asks, "Wouldn't it be easier if we got help from the teacher?" She isn't really asking a question at all; she is stating that she believes it would be a good idea to get help.

As part of our socialization, we learn that questions are a less demanding way of stating a preference, making a judgment, or of seeking a new course of action. And generally, most people understand these kinds of conventions and that they actually might smooth social interactions. Sometimes however, these conventions actually hinder good communication, and questions do so in at least two ways.

First, questions can be a withdrawal from the "rapport bank," the moment-to-moment emotional investment in the communication process itself. They often make the person being questioned feel defensive, and that defensiveness triggers reptilian feelings. As a result, the lines of communication shut down. But why do questions contribute to defensiveness? The answer lies in the underlying structure of language.

All native speakers of a language understand that there are a number of levels of communication happening at once. Although these layers of meaning may not be obvious to someone who is communicating in his or her second language, they are nevertheless the way we communicate subtle shades of meaning, as well as the cause of difficulties in translation. For instance, if someone asks, "Do you think our young children need to see all this violence on television?" native speakers understand that the person isn't really asking if children need to witness more violence. In fact, native speakers realize that it isn't even a real question at all.

In the course of conversation, questions communicate numerous subtle shades of meaning, judgment, and opinion. Because native speakers understand these deep structure meanings, they know when a question is really a judg-

> **FACTOID** Noam Chomsky was one of the first to introduce the idea that for people to understand any sentence, they also have to understand the underlying presuppositions, what he called the *deep structure* of the language (Caron, 1992). Sometimes, the deep structure is contextual; for instance the sentence, "Ship sails tonight," has a different meaning depending on the presuppositions of the deep structure. Is this an announcement of a boat embarking, or is it a directive from the manager of the marina to the night staff about sending some sails to a customer?

ment. The real difficulty arises when someone asks a question such as, "Do you really think it's a good idea to hand that in without typing it first?" The listener knows a judgment has been made, but at the same time, a question presupposes that an answer will be given. The defensiveness results because the person knows that the answer will be dismissed as wrong even before he or she gives it. It is like a husband asking his wife, "Are you really going to wear that dress to dinner tonight?" She has it on! Of course, she is going to be defensive (and probably angry, too.) Because so many questions are of this type— often as attempts to be gentle or nondemanding, sometimes to manipulate—people experience a twinge of defensiveness with many questions, even when they are simple, straightforward requests for information.

One strategy for dealing with questions that are really statements, opinions, or judgments is very powerful. Reflectively listen to the underlying statement. Instead of answering the question, respond to the deep structure. So, if someone asks the nonquestion, "Don't you think we have to start the project by Tuesday?" the listening response could simply be, "You are worried that if we don't start by Tuesday, we'll be in trouble."

Questions get in the way of good listening in a second way. Questions focus the mind, direct the thinking, and control the course of the conversation. When anyone asks a question (whether it is a real question or not), it focuses the mind, and once that happens, the questioner is charting the course of the conversation.

Activities for Teaching Listening

Good reflective listening is primarily a cognitive skill. After all, Steps 1 through 3 of the process are really invisible to everyone except the listener; it is only Step 4, the actual testing, that is overt. For that reason, teaching listening actually requires the teaching of thinking. To create readiness and for students to understand the importance of forming and testing hypotheses through feedback, the teacher might want to divide the *listening unit* into four broad sections:

I. Introduction of the listening cycle

    A. Activities for recognizing the importance of feedback

    B. The distinction between *everyday listening* and *reflective listening*

    C. Three steps versus four steps

II. Teacher modeling and guided practice

III. Recognizing and managing reactive responses

IV. Independent practice and ongoing feedback in small groups or cooperative learning teams

Once the students understand the steps and basic processes of reflective listening, there are many classroom and small group strategies for having the students practice their listening skills. In addition, these structures also shape classroom climate and set norms and expectations for the learning community

One of these structures is called *Paraphrase Passport*. During class discussion, or even when the teacher is calling on students to answer questions, each student must listen to and then reflect what the student just before has said (and get a confirming "yes" from that student) before he or she can give his or her answer. The benefits of Paraphrase Passport are numerous. In addition to providing reflective listening practice, it encourages students to stay focused, it establishes norms of respect and understanding, and it helps ensure that students attend and pay attention to each other. Also, Paraphrase Passport helps the functioning of cooperative learning groups. Because listening is the first step in just about all conflict management strategies, it helps establish small-group social norms for team learning. Moreover, it at least begins to help students see that different points of view can coexist, and it lays the foundation for tolerance and civility. Listening in the classroom, in small groups and in cooperative learning teams, is a powerful way to help students develop their emotional literacy.

Another strategy is one called *Corners*. This strategy is appropriate for just about any grade level or content, and because it involves getting up and moving around the room a little, it is a favorite of students. The first step in Corners is to have the students each make a forced choice between four or five options. In first grade, for instance, the students might be asked to pick their favorite sea animal: sharks, sea horses, whales, or dolphins. At the high school level, the teacher might focus on the key factors that contribute to just about anything— from the causes of a social problem to the reasons why one author is better than another. Once the students have made their individual choices, each student moves to the corner of the room designated for his or her choice. (In some classes and at some grade levels, the teacher might want the students to make their choices in writing so that they don't just go to the corner where their friends are.) Once the students are in their corners, the next step is to have pairs of listening buddies reflect each other's reasons for choosing that corner. Here, as in all good listening, the first goal is to understand the other person and get a confirming yes, which lets the listener know that the speaker is satisfied that the listener understands accurately. The third step is to have a few students report what their listening partners said. Again, this is a good way to establish the expectations and norms for listening.

Initially, the teacher may want to have students practice listening in this basic Corners structure. Later, when the students have had more listening experience, the teacher can have the students do more challenging work. In advanced Corners, the first couple of steps remain the same. Students make a choice, go to the appropriate corner, and practice listening with someone who agrees with them. Next, however, the teacher has students reflectively listen to those who don't agree with their answers. This can be done in a number of ways, and it is probably a good idea to use different strategies over time just for variety and to hold student interest.

One variation would be to create new listening teams made up of one person from each corner. The students might be asked to come to an agreement on a group statement that each of the members can support. The process of reaching that agreement would be an excellent way for the students to understand, appreciate, and practice good communication and emotional skills.

Students could also pair up with someone from a different corner. As a listening pair, the two students could prepare a mock debate, but each student would be supporting the other person's position. Again, such exchanges, especially when dealing with issues that trigger strong emotion, provide wonderful opportunities for students to stretch their skills.

In yet another variation, the teacher could direct a large classroom discussion by forecasting that some students will be called on to reflect what the speaker has just said, but that the listener will be called on from a different corner. Again, each of these strategies brings students a step closer to the goal of high emotional literacy through skilled, practiced listening.

It is ironic that most people who want to improve their communication skills look for some way to be better so-called communicators instead of better listeners. It may be a measure of their level of emotional literacy and of their relationship skills that they even conceive of the challenge first as a question of how to better get their ideas across instead of being more skilled at understanding others. Good listening is the beginning step. Without doubt, good listening is a hallmark of emotional literacy.

Summary

Some researchers claim that most spouses do real, empathetic listening with their partners for as little as 7 minutes each week. Children, who are just learning the skills and the effects of listening and being listened to, receive even less time each week.

Reflective listening is a rigorous skill that requires the listener to practice high-level emotional literacy by withholding his or her own mental rehearsal while seeking to truly understand the speaker. This skill can be broken into discrete steps and can be practiced in and out of the classroom.

This chapter addresses the behaviors and filters that can block good listening, called *reactive responses*. It also examines some of the gender differences in our predilection toward certain responses while we are listening to another person.

7

Nonverbal Cues

The Dance of Silent Communication

Contents

- The power of nonverbal cues in all communication
- Strategies for increasing sensory acuity
- Defining and recognizing the characteristics of rapport
- Introduction of pacing as an emotional literacy skill

Calibration is the key to successful communication.

—Genie Z. Laborde

Since the 1980s, Paul Ekman, professor of psychology at the University of California in San Francisco, has been studying nonverbal communication in humans (e.g., Ekman, 1997; Ekman & Davidson, 1998). His research includes cross-cultural investigations of the ability of people from different parts of the world to interpret facial expressions. He has worked with modern and primitive cultures, and he has found that you can show photos of a furious person or a miserable one from any culture to a person from a widely varying culture, and there will be no problem in understanding the emotion expressed. According to a *Psychology Today* article (Rotter, 1998),

Everyone makes the same face and everyone gets the message. . . . Researchers have identified six basic or universal expressions that appear to be hard wired in our brains, both to make and read: anger, fear, sadness, disgust, surprise and happiness. (p. 34)

In fact, George Rotter, a professor of psychology at Montclaire University, suggests in the same article that "the abilities to express and recognize emotion [nonverbally] are inborn, genetic, evolutionary" (p. 35).

> Gestures, facial expressions, posture, and the intensity and length of eye contact are of course influenced by culture. In fact, there are some societies that signal a nonverbal "No," by nodding. And at the same time, there are many nonverbal expressions that seem to be universal.

FACTOID Researchers have currently isolated "six basic or universal facial expressions":

- Anger
- Fear
- Sadness
- Disgust
- Surprise
- Happiness

A seventh may be embarrassment.

Of course, although it is true that there is probably no universal lexicon of nonverbal communication that could be the basis for a body language dictionary, it is also important to recognize that we all constantly assess the nonverbal signals that we receive to better understand each other. Because culture, upbringing, and developmental and emotional factors influence the ability to make and read these kinds of signals, some people seem more attuned to understanding others and more successful in expressing themselves. This ability is a significant hallmark of emotional literacy.

In this chapter, we will explore the fundamentals of nonverbal communication to help students and others become more conscious of and further develop these fundamental skills of emotional literacy.

Virginia Satir (1988) once put the number of nonverbal signals that influence us at 200 signals per second. It would be impossible for a person to attend to all of these signals consciously, so much of the influence of these nonverbals is subtle and outside of our immediate awareness. We certainly take these cues into account when we talk with people. Sometimes, we even prioritize signals. If a person is saying the words, "I'm fine, I'm fine," but is crying at the same time, we believe the nonverbal signals.

Some aspects of nonverbal communication are easy to identify; facial expression, gesture, posture, eye contact—even rate and depth of breathing are nonverbal signals. But technically, nonverbal communication extends to any part of the communication that is not the words themselves and their strict denotation. This means of course that for as long as teachers have taught students to read, they have been teaching many of the nuances of what is technically nonverbal expression—tone of voice, volume, emotional timbre, rate, as well as the number and length of pauses. All these and more combine to form a powerful subtext to the words. It is this subtext that actually shapes the ultimate meaning and intention the hearer understands.

For some, this process is particularly difficult. Abused children, for instance, are poised to detect threat even when it isn't there. Although this may be a useful compensating behavior that may protect them at home, it will likely lead to problems in school, in their friendships, and in their general emotional connection and relationships with others. Bullies, for instance—as either children or adults— tend to misread the nonverbal signals of others. The tendency to interpret ambiguous or even supportive signals as threatening or hostile is often a prelude to downshifting and ultimately to the damage to friendships, team work, and relationships of all kinds. In school, at work, and at home, the ability to make and read nonverbal signals is also the ability to manage relationships so that communication is accurate, positive, healthy, and caring.

If words are the content of the communication, nonverbal signals are the media, and just as there can be static on the line that interferes with communication on the telephone, so too, poor nonverbal communication can distort the message that is being sent when we are face to face. So then, what are some of the characteristics of successful nonverbal communication? What is it that people with high degrees of emotional literacy do that enable them to establish rapport?

Most people have had the experience of meeting someone and within just a few minutes feeling as if the two of them had a world of things in common. Communication was easy, almost as if there were some unspoken language between them. There is a name for this unspoken language. Scientists studying this phenomenon refer to *rapport* as a psychological state where the participants focus on the ideas, feelings, and content of their communication with little concern about acceptance or about the means of the communication itself. The ideas, words, and communication just seem to flow.

Socioanthropologists such as Desmond Morris find that there are many nonverbal signals that are correlated to this psychological state (Gregory, 1987). A subtle nonverbal dance takes place that communicates openness, acceptance, and interest. When these signals are sent, the receiver is likely to respond, even though he or she will probably be unaware consciously that the signals are there at all. For instance, there is a class of nonverbal signals that some refer to as *passive acknowledging responses* (some of our friends call them "animal noises"). These passive responses are subtle sounds people make that send the message that they are interested and paying attention. They include things like "uh ha," "hmm," "gee," and "okay." It is interesting that there is no single answer to the question,

> *Rapport* is a short-term psychological state where the participants focus on the ideas, feelings, and content of their communication with little concern about acceptance nor about the means of communication itself. The ideas, words, and communication just seem to flow. It is often characterized by mutual goals of connection and empathy.

> A *psychological state* is a short-term emotional and physiological response to some stimuli. For instance, we are conditioned to feel fear when in the presence of certain environmental cues. Movie makers use these cues to frighten us. Fortunately, psychological states usually last only as long as the stimuli are present.

Art Costa (1991; Costa & Garmston, 1994) may be the person who first coined the phrase, *animal noises*, in a Thinking Skills/Cognitive Coaching workshop. I am sure that he is one of the finest teachers of thinking and coaching and therefore of emotional literacy in the world.

"How often should we make these kinds of sounds if we want the listener to know we are attending?" First, because these kinds of subtle, out-of-consciousness signals are contextual, the number and frequency of these kinds of signals will vary. Second, there are individual differences that account for why one person might send or need more or fewer of these nonverbal cues. But although these differences may vary widely from person to person and circumstance to circumstance, one thing is clear: If the listener withholds all such signals, almost all speakers will become self-conscious, uneasy, and any chance for rapport building will be dramatically decreased.

FACTOID Pacing may have gotten its name from a phenomenon that occurs when we walk with another person. People generally like to be *in step* with each other when they walk.

There are other powerful nonverbal cues that indicate to researchers that rapport is strong or building. Scientists use the degree that two people are mirroring, or *pacing*, each other's gestures, body language, facial expressions, tempo, and posture as a measure of the strength of the rapport between them. The more that the participants match, the greater the rapport.

This sense of connection may be due in part to the congruence between each person's internal feelings, his or her *response state* and the outward physiology—breathing, expressions, posture (as well as the other nonverbal body language cues) that they are each sending. As the concepts and ideas—the content— are exchanged verbally, there is another language of emotional response to the content that is sent nonverbally. Obviously, if there is significant agreement on this level, communication will be more open and supportive, and there is a significant increase in the likelihood for rapport to develop.

Of course, the cues for pacing are completely natural. In fact, even infants respond to the signals or lack of signals from their mothers. In a study conducted by Jeffrey Cohen (as cited in Rotter, 1998, p. 78) at the University of Pittsburgh, mothers were told not to smile at their babies as they held them. At first, the infants tried to elicit a response from the mother. But the infants simply could not continue to interact without receiving a response. They stopped their efforts, mirroring the detached expression of their mothers. And even though the experiment lasted only 3 minutes, the babies remained distant for up to a minute after the mothers resumed normal behavior.

The implications of this kind of research are dramatic and far-reaching. There are children who come from homes where, because of depression, illness, or some other cause, positive, nurturing nonverbal feedback is rare or absent. For these children, the fundamental mechanisms for learning how to make connections, foster communication, and establish rapport are lacking. Without specific interventions, these young people may never be as successful in their relationships as others.

In addition, the research on the nonverbal cues of communication point out that the question of whether we are going to use these cues is irrelevant. We cannot avoid sending such signals. The only real question is whether we will be able to consciously and skillfully master these powerful, natural communication cues.

Last, this research reminds us that the rules for being a good listener that we learn in primary school may not be as universal as we once thought. Just as there are individual differences in the communication styles of people, so too different cultural norms influence the nonverbal cues that are appropriate and useful. Some researchers, such as Deborah Tannen (1990), even isolate differences in the signals used by men and women. If there is no universal lexicon that we can refer to so that we send the right signals, then where are we to look?

The single most powerful finding to come out of this research is simply this: Attend to the nonverbal cues that the other person is sending, use those signals as feedback, and then match, or mirror, those cues.

There are four key concepts to teach when working with students to help them develop pacing skills. First, students should understand, through some kind of experiential learning, that the processes of rapport building are completely natural and that in fact they already do

> Sensory acuity refers to the degree to which a person is sensitive to the feedback cues and other nonverbal signals that another person is sending. People with high emotional literacy tend to have high sensory acuity. They are good at reading the subtle, nonverbal cues of others.

these things unconsciously every day. Second, as students begin to purposely practice rapport-building techniques, they should understand the subtleness of the cues. Pacing is never mocking or imitating; instead it is a slow, respectful mirroring. Third, students should receive practice in developing *sensory acuity*; that is, they should become progressively more conscious of the nonverbal cues that others are sending. Fourth, students should develop an understanding and an appreciation of the interactive nature of the communication feedback cycle.

By approaching these four key concepts individually, the next section offers suggestions and teaching strategies so that students can, with practice, integrate their understanding and form a solid foundation for enhancing their communication skills.

> *Four Key Pacing Concepts*
> 1. Pacing is *a natural part of the communication process.*
> 2. Pacing is *a subtle interaction*, never mocking.
> 3. Practice is required in order to develop *sensory acuity.*
> 4. Skillful communicators rely on important cues they receive in the *continuous communication feedback cycle.*

Approaches to Developing Nonverbal Communication Skills

The first step in developing the ability to establish rapport is to have the students become conscious of pacing as a skill, in the first place. One way to accomplish this is something called a *Freeze Frame*. In this activity, the teacher suggests a topic and has the students engage in a structured, one-on-one dialogue with another student. Because some topics are more likely to foster rapport than others, the choice of topic in this activity is very important. For instance, asking students to tell their partner about a person who has had a powerful, positive impact on them will promote natural rapport for most people. Almost any exchange where the students share some *positive events or experiences that they have in common* can be the basis for a Freeze Frame. Before the students start talking, the teacher should forecast that he or she will be moving around the room and might interrupt some people now and then.

> The *communication feedback cycle* is a reinforcing loop that develops when one person attends to the cues that another person is sending. By paying attention and responding appropriately to these signals, the emotionally skilled person is able to deepen rapport, foster good communication, and to build trust.

While the students are engaged, the teacher watches for clear examples of pacing. When the teacher sees, for instance, that two students have established mirrored postures, he or she may approach them and interrupt them, asking that they freeze right where they are.

Next, the teacher will point out the obvious similarities in the body language, posture, and the overall mirroring and symmetry between the two. Last, he or she can ask the students to "tuck this observation away" so the students are aware later of the specific details of their mirroring. It is also useful to invite the pair to briefly scan the room to find other examples of mirroring in other pairs before returning to their conversation. After identifying a number of these freeze

> The *T-Chart* is a graphic that can be used to teach specific skills. To use a T-chart, the teacher identifies (or has the students identify) specific observable target behaviors that indicate that the skill is being used. The behaviors are categorized by what an observer would see and hear. Here is an example of a T-Chart:
>
> ### Skillful Pacing for Rapport
>
> | Looks like | Sounds like |
> |---|---|
> | • Mirroring gestures | • Same volume |
> | • Matching smiles | • Matching tone |
> | • Mirroring nodding | • Laughing together |
> | • Matching posture | • Talking same speed |
> | • Mirroring | • Using same words |

frames, the teacher can then introduce the concepts of rapport and pacing and ask the students to report their own data as specific examples that can be analyzed.

As a result of this introduction, three important learning objectives can be met. First, students will be able to describe and find examples of pacing from their own experience. Second, students will be able to refer to their own experience to support the fact that pacing occurs naturally. Last, students will be more conscious of what rapport and pacing are, and they will be able to explain what had been for them an out-of-consciousness phenomenon.

The second step in the learning process is to have students consciously practice rapport-building skills. In this phase, the teacher has many options: T-charts can be used to isolate specific pacing skills and to identify those skills in terms of concrete behaviors. For instance, a T-chart for pacing for rapport might, on one side, have some of the sounds a listener might make—animal noises, for example. On the other side of the T-chart, the teacher could list some of the specific body language matching that might occur. By having a T-chart, the students have a benchmark. Focusing on a few concrete behaviors at a time, the students will be able to add to their repertoire over time.

Another strategy that focuses student practice is called *Chips in the Middle.* In this technique, each student is given some number of *pacing chips.* As students work in pairs on some academic task, they are also responsible for practicing the specific kinds of pacing that are named on their chips. As they practice their skills, they put one of their chips on the table to signify that they remembered, they were conscious of practicing, and that they succeeded.

Another variation with chips is *Catch Someone Being a Pacer.* Here, the teacher passes out pacing chips, but for this activity, students are asked to be on the lookout for other students practicing rapport-building skills. When one child catches another being a pacer, he or she gives that child a chip with the particular pacing technique listed on it. In this way, students are encouraged to be conscious of the nonverbal signals of others.

In addition to fostering heightened consciousness and sensory acuity, this activity also encourages students to decode other students' nonverbal responses to being paced. Although students are on the lookout so they can give chips to others, they also observe and give each other feedback about how another student's listening partner responded to pacing. So although Linda and Mary are working on a way to solve a math problem, Bruce might be on the lookout for pacing. When Bruce sees that Mary is responding to Linda's pacing, he could pay attention to Mary's nonverbal reactions and responses. Then he might give Linda a pacing chip. This variation for using chips reinforces at least three goals because it helps the students the following ways:

1. Develops heightened consciousness to nonverbal cues
2. Internalizes rapport-building skills
3. Cultivates awareness of the self-reinforcing nature of feedback loops in communication processes

Another somewhat advanced strategy is a kind of game that students both benefit from and enjoy. The object of the game is for one student—the observer— to identify what his or her partner is remembering, just by paying attention to nonverbal cues! In the activity, there are two partners. These are the steps:

1. One partner identifies in his or her mind three powerful experiences from the past. When the students first start playing, the teacher should instruct the students that the three experiences should be quite different from one another. (As the students gain greater sensory acuity, the remembered experiences can be more similar.)
2. Then, without speaking, this same student recalls as vividly as possible one of the events. He or she should allow him or herself to recall how the event felt and what his or her emotions were at the time. He or she should even be encouraged to recall the sights and sounds of that moment in time.
3. As the student is recalling the event, the observer watches for and mentally notes the posture, facial expressions, breathing, and all other nonverbal signals he or she can.
4. After a few moments, the first student takes a moment to stretch and then recalls the second event, again focusing on the same kinds of vivid details as the first.
5. Again, the observer watches for, makes mental notes of, and begins to calibrate the nonverbal cues to each of the two recollections.

6. The first student again takes a moment to stretch, so that there is a clear break in the nonverbal cues, and then repeats the procedure with the third event.
7. Now, they are ready to play. The first student randomly picks one of the three events, without telling the other student if it is the first, second, or third.
8. The observing student now tries to identify which of the three he or she is seeing. If he or she gets it wrong, the first student will disclose which event it was by identifying it as the first, second, or third event. (There is no need to tell the details of the event being recalled.) Then, the observing student gets another opportunity to attend to the nonverbal cues more precisely. The goal is for the observing student to correctly identify four instances in a row.
9. After a few rounds, the players switch roles so that they both have practice developing their sensory acuity. The only other ground rule is that the student who is recalling the events is to behave naturally. He or she shouldn't try to hide his or her nonverbal cues nor mislead the observer.

Most students find this a fascinating activity. It can become one of the students' favorites and has numerous applications. Once students begin to develop sensory acuity to nonverbal signals, they will also be developing greater consciousness in all aspects of communications. Ultimately, this greater awareness can lead to greater flexibility.

As students look at the skills that make a difference in their abilities to communicate, we hope they will gain a greater appreciation of the many subtle cues that are exchanged moment by moment. Consciousness of and respect for the power of nonverbal communication can lead to a profound affect on the way students interact with others.

Summary

From birth, we mirror and repeat the nonverbal messages we receive from others. In these earliest stages, we are developing a significant skill basic to emotional literacy. When these skills are not modeled or reinforced, they do not develop and leave the person less equipped to send and receive communication.

Becoming expert at noticing the nonverbal signals in others (increasing our sensory acuity) and using that data as feedback to inform our next communication creates rapport and trust in a relationship. This also improves our ability to communicate with that person well.

Students can develop specific skills in increasing their own sensory acuity, in pacing for rapport, and in consciously using nonverbal feedback.

8

Maintaining Important Relationships

Assertion and Apology

Contents

- The task relationship grid
- The assertion sequence
- The attributes of a successful apology

We are our choices.

Jean-Paul Sartre

No matter what, there will be times when things go wrong, even in the best relationships. Because we are most vulnerable in those very relationships we most cherish, these are also the relationships that are most susceptible to damage when someone oversteps a boundary. Misunderstandings, missteps, and trespasses that cross the peripheries of self and other are simply a reality. Given the inevitability of these challenges, it would seem that we would have lots of opportunities to learn how to pilot these difficult emotional rapids. Unfortunately for many young people and adults alike, the most common strategies—fight or flight—

actually cause more long-term harm than good. After a few unhappy experiences, many people resort to simple avoidance of the potential conflict—a flight behavior—or they take the aggressive—fight—approach.

In any case, unless we consciously choose a strategy that matches our desired outcomes,

> *Assertion* and *apology* are two communication templates for handling the difficult times when someone has trespassed over some boundary. They help protect both the relationship and the boundaries.

> *Fight* and *flight* are the two extremes of the reptilian survival response. Because the physiological charge that readies our bodies for conflict is so powerful, we often react with almost total disregard for the long-term consequences of our actions. Understanding the nature of these responses can help us be more forgiving of ourselves and of others.

we are at the mercy of a part of the brain that is just not very good at maintaining relationships, problem solving, or even clearly articulating our underlying interests. The reptilian behaviors are focused on the most basic forms of survival, not on being emotionally smart. *Assertion* and *apology* are two templates to help our students and ourselves protect, maintain, and even strengthen our relationships. At first, they could be considered basic coping strategies. As students become more and more emotionally literate, they will develop additional strategies. But no matter how skilled they become, these templates will always offer two useful alternatives in times of stress.

Relationship-Task Grid

To fully understand the implications and the consequences of their choices, students should understand the range of choices that they have. Then, and perhaps only then, can students really appreciate and take responsibility for their relationship decisions. Most of us have

The Assertion Continuum

Both ends of the assertion continuum are marked by the extremes of the reptilian response.

At the aggressive side, we see behaviors that actually reflect prehistoric strategies for establishing dominance: puffing up, loudness, large gestures and movement, intense eye contact—what some have referred to as "in your face" behaviors.

At the other end, we see behaviors of submission: cowering, little or no eye contact, looking down, small or no physical movement, quiet voice. What both of these sets of behavior share is this: By definition, they are both irrational; they are generated from that part of the brain that does not cope with life in a deliberate, cognitive manner.

Passive Behaviors   Aggressive Behaviors

|———————————————————————————|

Assertion is an entirely different kind of approach. It is a conscious choice that is made with clear cognitive outcomes in mind. It both protects the relationship and, at the same time, maintains appropriate boundaries.

never had the opportunity to actually assess what these choices might be. In fact, many actually make no choices at all; they are locked into a set of inflexible behaviors, either because they lack a particular communication skill or template or they are unaware that they have choices at all. Once a person becomes conscious of his or her choices, he or she moves a step closer to emotional literacy.

One of the clearest ways to represent the possible choices in a relationship is through the *relationship-task grid* (see Figure 8.1).

The first axis on the grid represents concern for maintaining a relationship; the second axis represents concern for tasks or boundaries in the relationship. By examining the possibilities for locations on the grid, students can begin to map various relationships that they already have and also begin taking responsibility for the choices they make in the future.

One possible position on the grid is located in the high relationship-low task quadrant. Here, the choice is characterized by *accommodation:* an almost unmitigated concern for protecting the relationship at nearly any cost. A person in this position is likely to continue to collapse boundaries for the sake of the relationship. Although this is not necessarily a bad choice under some circumstances, it can be self-defeating and dysfunctional if it becomes a habit.

Rapport is a short-term psychological state in which people feel that the lines of communication are wide open. At a time of deep rapport, the people involved have nearly all of their conscious thought processes focused on what they have to say, instead of on aspects of the relationship. They often will feel safe, comfortable, secure, and accepted.

At the other extreme is the low relationship-high task position. This choice is often described as one of great control. The person here

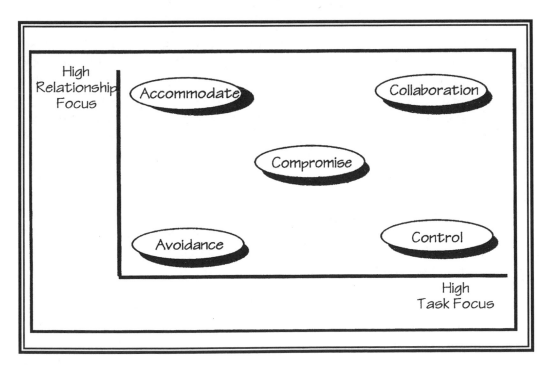

Figure 8.1. The Relationship Task Grid

Generally, task concerns are short term. Sooner or later, the deadline will pass, the job will be finished, the project will be over.

On the other hand, relationship concerns tend to be long term. Months after the project is over, we still remember how we were treated, even if we don't remember the exact circumstances of the task that caused the stress in the first place.

generally *sacrifices other's feelings and needs in order to have his or her own needs and boundaries satisfied.* Certainly, there are times of imminent danger or crisis that make this position not only understandable but actually appropriate and desirable. If, however, a person's choices are limited to this position, whether out of lack of skill or awareness, it can, in the extreme, lead to relationships that are abusive, damaging, and doomed to failure.

For each of us, there are pressures that tend to push us in one direction or the other on the grid. After all, if there are no relationship stresses nor task stresses, it is easy to maintain the balance between the two extremes. A first step for students may be for them to reflect on their own tendencies and to understand the kinds of pressures that tend to drive their choices.

And there are at least three other general locations on the grid to choose from: low relationship-low task, high relationship-high task, and the center ground that is equidistant from both relationship and task. Understanding the dynamics of each of these positions leads to deeper understanding of the choices we have in all relationships.

The low-low or avoidance position is characterized by almost complete withdrawal from both task and relationship. This is where we might be when we really don't care about the other people who are involved in a task, and we don't care about the project, either! This might also be the place a person might go to if he or she has taken trusting steps in the past but has been hurt. Now, he or she compensates by refusing to care. A student in this position will openly demonstrate that he or she doesn't care about other kids in the group and doesn't care about getting the work done, either. From a certain perspective, this seems like a pretty safe place to be: If you don't care at all about any aspect of what your group is doing, you don't risk failure, and there isn't much that can happen to hurt you.

The high-high or collaborative position is in some ways the most demanding. To be consciously aware of the needs of others and at the same time manage the demands of getting the work done or protecting one's own interests takes great emotional intelligence. Certainly, the greater the demands on one side, the harder it is to balance the other. It is a daunting charge, and without access to the kinds of skills we've examined so far, it may be almost impossible. Yet there are many people who demonstrate this *grace under pressure:* Even when the stress of the task is great, they have the skills to manage themselves and their relationships in an emotionally literate way. In most long-term relationships, the high relationship-high task quadrant is the most productive in the long run. This position is characterized by collaborative problem solving, by shared vision of goals and mission, and by win-win solutions that focus on meeting the underlying interests of all.

Even with these generally positive features to its credit, this approach is not necessarily appropriate in all situations. First, this approach assumes that the relationship will be a long term one. Win-win and collaborative problem solving only work when all parties recognize that they will be working together in the future; otherwise, there is a much greater likelihood that one party will take advantage of the other. If a salesperson is never going to see this customer again, then there is very little investment in the relationship. Some unscrupulous people will go to the low relationship-high task quadrant and manipulate the customer by *pretending to care about the relationship* for the sole purpose of exploiting him or her.

FACTOID *Grace under pressure* may be a good indicator of a person's emotional literacy. Students in cooperative learning groups, on teams, and in other relationships must always balance the demands of the task with the demands of the relationship. On the task side, there are deadlines, schedules, expectations, and standards that must be met. On the relationship side, time must be invested to foster good communication, to create commitment and win-win solutions, to manage territory issues, and to manage the predictable human responses to change.

Last, there is the middle ground of compromise. Whereas the upper right position is characterized by win-win collaboration, the mid-

FACTOID We often hear relationships or even people described as "dysfunctional." Yet, the term is misunderstood by most people. Derived from the Latin, "dys" suggests not only the idea of *bad or poor functioning*, but it also suggests the *pain of disease.* In a sense then, the word *dysfunction* should remind us that the person or the relationship is not only functioning poorly but also that the person is functioning the best he or she can while in great pain.

dle position is marked by what must ultimately be seen as a kind of lose-lose negotiation. Certainly in one sense, compromise often leads to the best possible outcome, given the time, level of commitment, and the underlying interests of the negotiating parties. In another sense, however, the word *compromise* means to make concessions; in still another, it means to sacrifice. So as long as we both concede and sacrifice some things that are important, we have compromise. In a long-term relationship, if compromise becomes the norm, the things being sacrificed are the high commitments to both relationship and task. We may end up settling for a weaker alliance.

Whatever we end up with, however, should be a conscious choice. There are times and circumstances that justify each of the possibilities in the relationship-task grid. The keys for students, and for all of us, must be *awareness* and *responsibility*. Many people accommodate because they do not recognize that they have other choices or because they don't know how to do anything else. The same is true for each of the positions. A bullying boss may get the short-term task finished in time, but if he or she has no options other than low relationship control, then he or she is limited not only in the ability to lead but also in the ability to maintain adaptive, flexible, long-term relationships. There are even times when a low-low avoidance approach really is the most emotionally savvy choice. But children who learn this strategy to compensate for an abusive or neglectful home life often generalize the approach to all relationships. Even if it worked to protect the child at some point in his or her life, it will probably be a painful journey for the adult who never develops any other options.

Just as we are ultimately responsible for all of our choices, we are responsible, too, for the relationships we help create. Understanding the contexts, goals, and characteristics of different kinds of relationships and understanding the dynamics of our relationship choices helps us to make the kinds of distinctions that indicate emotional literacy. The choices we make influence the quality of our relationships and of our lives.

One place where these kinds of choices have the greatest impact is when someone has violated a relationship or individual norm, boundary, or value. From what we already know about the downshifting and dynamics of the reptilian response and from what we know about the dynamics illustrated in the relationship-task grid, it is easy to understand that these times are very trying, even for the most emotionally literate. The more we equip students and ourselves with concrete strategies to handle these difficult relationship intervals, the more we foster flexibility, adaptivity, and relationship success.

The task-relationship grid can be used in a number of ways. As a *diagnostic tool*, it can provide students with five specific relationship models. Of course, the number of variations to these basic five are infinite, but as a template, it provides a foundation for students to use as they look at their own relationships. The grid can also be a kind of lens for students to use as they examine themselves and the roles they tend to take in their relationships.

FACTOID

In addition to using the relationship-task grid to help students understand the dynamics of their own relationships, it can also be used as a tool to help students analyze other relationships. There are obvious applications in English classes where students can examine the motives and relationship tendencies of fictional characters, but other subjects could benefit as well. Combined with an understanding of interest-based negotiation and reframing, students can apply this information to the political and economic relationships they study in social studies.

The Assertion Sequence

The *assertion sequence* is a specific communication strategy for communicating two things simultaneously:

> *Downshifting*
>
> Downshifting involves significant neural energy focused on fight-or-flight reptilian responses. It doesn't leave much room for carefully thinking or problem solving.

1. A boundary or norm has been violated and that must be addressed

2. This relationship is important and must not be sacrificed

> The *assertion sequence* describes the predictable sequence of steps that usually occurs when one person asserts to another. Generally, when the assertion is made, it will probably trigger downshifting. The person being asserted to will try to escape from or refocus the conversation in order to avoid having to deal with the first person's assertion. What happens next in the sequence is determined by the asserter's skill.

Unfortunately, many people don't have a template or strategy for balancing both of these simultaneous concerns. As a result, they either tend toward high relationship-low task, in which case the boundary is collapsed, or they tend toward low relationship-high task, where the boundary is protected, but the relationship suffers. The assertion sequence offers an opportunity to make the high relationship-high task choice.

To be fully prepared, the asserter must understand the assertion sequence, the asserter's role in it, and the importance of good reflective listening. The assertion sequence with its assertion statement is an important template for dealing with another person who has

> The person being asserted to will more likely respond with a push back. *Push backs are reactive responses to what the asserter says.* Once the push back occurs, the focus is taken off the assertion. Like all reactive responses, the push back interferes with the speaker expressing him or herself.

failed to respect an agreement, a value, or a boundary. It provides a structure for focusing on the one key issue while protecting the relationship from the kind of free-for-all arguments that often damage the relationship's long-term viability. In addition, by using the assertion template, both parties in the relationship learn

The asserter must practice good reflective listening skills when the person being asserted to pushes back. The listening will help the person upshift. Before the assertion is finished, the asserter will need to use his or her skills many times over.

FACTOID

Categories and Examples of Reactive Responses

Judging	1. Agreeing or disagreeing
	2. Criticizing or blaming
	3. Diagnosing
	4. Praising
Parenting and Solving	5. Ordering
	6. Threatening
	7. Moralizing
	8. Advising
	9. Questioning
	10. Problem solving
Avoiding	11. Logical Arguing
	12. Reassuring
	13. Diverting
	14. Understanding
	15. Joking

If a person decides that he or she is going to assert, it is absolutely vital that before beginning the assertion sequence, he or she must be prepared to stay focused and centered. Reframing, anchoring, and an understanding of downshifting can help the asserter maintain his or her emotional center. These same skills allow the asserter to pardon the other person's downshifting. For the sake of the relationship, the asserter must recognize that for a short time, the other person may behave emotionally and illogically. It is predictable, human, and pretty much universal.

that they will deal with the inevitable difficulties in a constructive, healthy, respectful manner.

Obviously, all relationships develop norms for how the people in them will deal with conflict, chaos, and trespasses. Assertion is a very productive way for individuals to learn to maintain appropriate boundaries and at the same time to balance the demands of the relationship. The really difficult part of the assertion sequence is managing this dance of the "difficult to say." However, this is possible when the person asserting uses the template and maintains his cognitive, higher-level thinking.

The actual assertion statement is fairly straightforward and simple. It contains at least two parts, and when possible, three.

The first part of the assertion statement is a description of the problem behavior. The description should be as objective as possible, free of judgments and criticism. For instance, "When there are dishes in the sink," is a clear description of fact. Another example might focus on a student's lack of responsibility to the members of his cooperative group. One of his teammates might say something like this: "When you forget to bring your homework to school, like today, . . ." Here again, there is an simple description of the fact that this or that happened.

The second required part of the assertion is the statement of feelings. The person making the assertion names his or her feelings to the other person. It may be a subtle distinction, but it is important that the student try to own his or her feelings and to refrain from blaming those feelings on the other person. There is a difference between saying, "When you forget your homework, you make me angry," and "When you forget your homework, I feel angry." In the first example, it is as if one person can control someone else's emotion. In the second, the person is providing information about his or her emotions within a specific context.

The third and only really optional part of the assertion is an explanation of the costs to the asserter. So for example, to say that I feel angry *because I end up unable to complete my own work on time* explains the impact of the other person's behavior. Here again, it is important to help the stu-

A typical *assertion statement* contains at least these two parts:

1. An objective description of the problem behavior
2. A statement of the speaker's feelings

An assertion may also include a third part that describes the tangible effects that the problem behavior brings to the asserter.

For example, "When you interrupt me when I am speaking, I feel very frustrated and angry because it becomes impossible for me to do my job."

dents learn the distinctions between a simple description of the effects of the other person's behavior and a statement that is judgmental and blaming. Taking this all into account, the student in the cooperative learning group might make his or her assertion in this way: "Bill, when you forget to bring in your homework, like today, I get really mad because I can't get my own work done on time."

A fundamental feature of the assertion sequence is a *series of emotional, reactive response spikes that occur each time the assertion is made.* The asserter must anticipate and be prepared to deal with his or her own downshifting, as well as the downshifting of the person who is on the receiving end of the assertion. In addition, the asserter must be able to practice reflective listening to help manage the volatility of the exchanges. The graph in Figure 8.2 illustrates the basic spike pattern. And although this is the basic component, the assertion sequence is made up of a series of these spikes. It is the *series* of spikes that really tests the asserter's emotional literacy.

The challenge for the asserter is to avoid his or her own downshifting. Push backs (the reactive response spikes) are likely to be very intense and very powerful, and because reactive responses tend to elicit downshifting in the other person, these interchanges require highly developed listening skills.

At least one of the people must be skilled or else a simple assertion regarding a small agreement, a *small* problem, can escalate into an

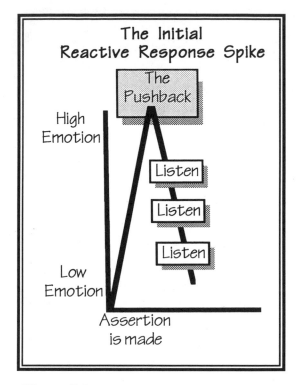

The Initial Reactive Response Spike

The Pushback

High Emotion

Listen

Listen

Listen

Low Emotion

Assertion is made

Figure 8.2.

awful, hurtful fight, where the two people actually cause great damage to the relationship in the moment, as well as crippling its ability to deal with future problems in a functional way.

As the person receiving the assertion pushes back, the asserter uses his or her reflective listening skills to lower the emotion and to send the message that he or she hears the assertee's point of view. As he or she listens, the asserter is watching for nonverbal cues, and for a "yes" from the other person that indicates that the person being asserted to recognizes that he or she is being heard.

Suppose, for instance, that Kathy makes the following assertion to Rob: "When there are dishes left in the sink, like right now, I get mad because if I want to use the kitchen, I have to clean it up first." A classic push back to this assertion might be, "I didn't do it. It wasn't me." (As push backs go, this one is often used pretty mindlessly, especially in this case, because no one else was home!) In school, kids say these kinds of things all the time: "I wasn't talking. Billy was talking to me." At home, kids say things like, "Don't blame me for the mess. It wasn't my glass."

In any case, Kathy must now deal with what she knows is a lie. What is fascinating about such a lie is that it is totally illogical. At some level, the person saying it understands that the other person knows it is a lie, yet he or she says it anyway. It may be a testament to the power of downshifting that a person will say or do almost anything, no matter how illogical, if it might work to help him escape from the assertion. The push back—whether it is a lie or an attempt to switch blame, or even if it is to cry—whatever the push back, it is a downshifted attempt to escape the assertion.

Still, the asserter must somehow deal with the push back. Generally, to confront it directly leads to an unraveling of the interaction.

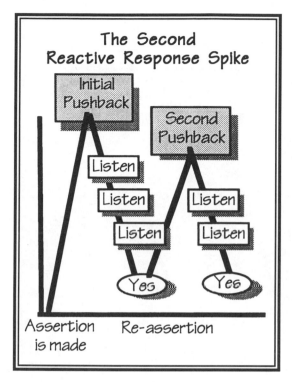

The Second Reactive Response Spike

Initial Pushback

Second Pushback

Listen

Listen   Listen

Listen   Listen

Yes   Yes

Assertion is made   Re-assertion

Figure 8.3.

If instead of staying focused on the particular issue, Kathy addresses the push back, then before they know it, the two people will be arguing about how truthful they each are, about other lies in the past, about whether either of them should ever have trusted the other one in the first place, and on and on. In most cases, this kind of free-for-all results in much greater damage than a dish in the sink ever could.

So how is Kathy supposed to deal with a statement that she very well knows is untrue? She practices reflective listening; she gets a "yes," and she restates her original assertion. The first part, the reflective listening, might sound like this:

> **Kathy:** When there are dishes left in the sink, like right now, I get mad because if I want to use the kitchen, I have to clean it up first.
>
> **Rob:** I didn't do it. It wasn't me.
>
> **Kathy:** So you're saying that you don't remember leaving the dishes there at all.
>
> **Rob:** Yeah, I mean I wouldn't just leave them there for you to do them.
>
> **Kathy:** You're saying that you wouldn't just leave them there, right?
>
> **Rob:** Right.

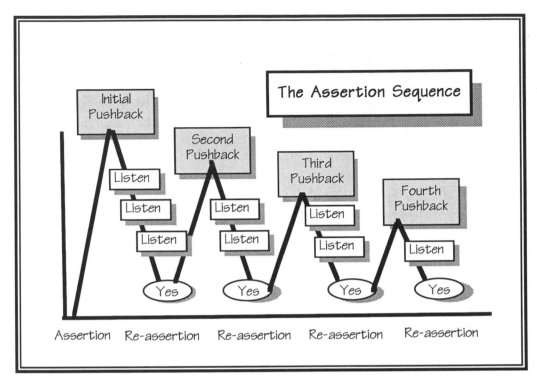

Figure 8.4.

Once Kathy gets this "yes" from Rob, she can then restate her original assertion, connecting it to the "yes" she's just received. It might sound like this:

Kathy: So as far as you can remember, the dishes aren't yours, and you wouldn't just leave them there for me *and I'm still stuck, because* when there are dishes in the sink, it really makes me angry because to use the kitchen, I have to spend my time cleaning up first.

The reassertion will, of course, trigger a new reptilian, reactive push back, which will require the asserter to listen and get a "yes." The "yes" is followed by yet another reassertion, and the process repeats itself. This may go on four or five times (see Figure 8.4).

The sequence ends when the conversation moves from excuses and push backs to an honest dialog about the issue itself. It is certainly tempting to delve into all of the other tangential push back issues, but the wiser path is probably to take time out to see if they really need to be discussed at all. Of course, real issues must be addressed, but often, push-back reactive responses are not real at all.

The Apology

Whereas the assertion sequence provides a template when one person must confront another, there are also times when, instead of a confrontation, an apology is the best tool to protect boundaries, values, and agreements, as well to maintain the relationship itself. When a person wants to repair the damage he or she has caused to a relationship, a simple, "I'm sorry," usually will not suffice. Because of the emotional vulnerability inherent in close relationships, if one party feels that the other has been untrustworthy, the very act of apology itself can be suspect. If the attempts to mend the relationship are to be successful, the apology must be compatible with what we know about the causes of downshifting and about the relationship-task grid.

Downshifting results from a perceived threat to some boundary. Because close relationships require us to be trusting, there is already a high degree of vulnerability. We feel unprotected, and it is only our faith in our mutual respect for these limits that keeps us feeling safe. When someone violates this understanding, they have in some way threatened the faith in our own safety. If we experience a loss of faith, an apology is only the first step in mending the relationship.

But it is an important first step because by seeking to make apology, we admit that we did something that hurt the other person and the relationship. By admitting that we did this, we also demonstrate our understanding of the trespass, and we give the power of the boundary back to the offended person. Now, we are the ones who must ask for the boundary to be maintained again. We make ourselves vulnerable to rejection, and we admit that it should be so. And the offended person always has the option to reject our apology.

The Attributes of a Meaningful Apology

An apology must contain at least four key components if it is to restore the boundaries and at the same time begin the healing of the relationship. First, the apologizer must accept blame for violating the norm or agreement. Second, the offender should explain that it was not an intentional disregard for what must be a shared value or norm. So as the person is admitting his or her mistake, at the same time, he or she should reinforce the commitment to the very principle that has been violated.

These first two components help establish the sanctity of the boundary. In terms of the relationship-task grid, the apologizer is demonstrating willingness to adhere to and be controlled by the very rule or rules that were broken. In addition, he or she is laying the foundation for the commitment to keeping his or her word in the future.

Third, the apology should communicate that any and all pain that was caused was also unintentional. In other words, the offense was not directed at the other person. To repair the relationship, the person apologizing must show understanding of the pain caused as well as concern about the possibility that having caused pain could result in the loss of the relationship itself. In this way, the apology reinforces both the boundaries of the relationship and the value of the individual.

Last, the apology should communicate regret, sorrow, and an appropriate sense of embarrassment. After all, the apology should admit the we did something we are ashamed of having done. It is important to express that the motives for the apology are sincere and that the apology itself is a reflection of a set of deeply held personal convictions.

The templates described in this chapter can help students and adults alike to cope with what may be one of the most challenging episodes in any relationship. Whenever there is a violation of a norm or agreement in a relationship, the relationship will be thrown into chaos. Unfortunately, chaos is a frightening place to be. Because of the our natural human tendencies, our instinctual responses may actually create even more hurt and confusion.

During such times, it is useful to have a map or two to help us navigate safely through the troubled waters.

Summary

We can frame our decisions around two key elements when dealing with other people. The first is concerned with the human relationship; it is the long-term element. The second is the task or work with which we are concerned; it is the short-term element because eventually it is completed or ends. When we make respectful decisions about our behaviors, we are conscious of both of these elements and of the consequences of not choosing to maintain both.

Sometimes, the emotionally literate person must confront another person who has not respected boundaries or agreements. The assertion sequence is a template for doing this respectfully yet clearly. At other times, a person may have neglected a boundary or agreement, and a clear, sincere apology is needed. Both assertion and apology are discussed in this chapter.

9

Learning From Experience

Self-Coaching

Contents

- Definition of the learning cycle
- Explanation of experiential learning
- Development of the attitude of a learner
- Strategies for teaching the learning cycle: Green magic

In the beginner's mind there are many possibilities; in the expert's mind there are few.

—Suzuki Roshi, *Zen Mind*

We are a species of learners; the impulse to learn is built into our brains as a result of millions of years of evolution. The evolutionary advantages of such learning are obvious: We are able to repeat those behaviors that are useful, and we are able to avoid behaviors that deter progress. Yet such learning is not easy nor is it guaranteed. Some people seem predisposed to learning from experience, others less so. In addition, the circumstances surrounding an experience can either contribute to or detract from the person's reflection and thus his or her learning from that experience. In this chapter, we explore what it means to self-coach and how this is related to learning from experience, to continuous growth, and to the development of the kinds of distinctions that lead to a repertoire of skills, tools, and maps that enhance emotional literacy.

Background

From the time when we lived in caves, there have been benefits directly connected to our ability to learn from experience; It is how we learned to avoid poison. For sure, at some time in our ancient past, we regularly ate things that made us sick. At some point, someone in the tribe made

> One key distinction that is characteristic of the very best thinkers, problem solvers, and decision makers is their ability to be metacognitive. A habit of mind, *metacognition* is the ability to think about one's own thinking and problem solving while actually thinking and problem solving. It represents executive control of the thinking processes themselves.

the connection between a certain patch of red berries and being sick. It was in the best interest of the community that this learning occurred. It is funny to imagine the tribal leaders testing this hypothesis by sending someone out to the berry patch to eat red berries. But after that person got sick once again, the rest of the tribe was able to make a distinction that made a difference. We do the same

> **FACTOID**
> Albert Einstein once defined insanity as "doing the same thing over and over again, but expecting a different outcome."

thing today; after one or two bad experiences at a restaurant, we don't go back.

On the other side of the coin, this learning from experience also helps us identify the causes of success, and this increases the likelihood that we'll repeat those behaviors in the future. Certainly, it was an advantage to our species that we were able to recognize and apply some prehistoric insights about pointed sticks being better than clubs

The Triune Brain

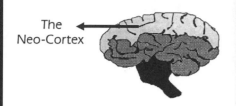

The
Neo-Cortex

It is likely that the neo-cortex is the center for the kind of executive control thinking associated with metacognition and self-coaching. This is the part of the brain that is correlated to rational, logical problem solving, to language and decision making. Some scientists believe that this part of the brain may in fact house not only the ability to predict the future consequences and outcomes of some choice, but also the means for making the choice at all.

for some tasks. Today, just as then, the predisposition to learn from our experiences increases our chances for success.

Coaches of all kinds help their players continue to improve by providing the time and opportunity for players to reflect on their playing, to process their experience, and then to form and use their insights to continually improve their performance.

So the team plays the basketball game on Friday. At the next practice, the coach has the kids watch the game tapes to identify those things that helped and those things that hindered success. Then he or she has the players work on specific skills so that their efforts are focused and mindfully directed toward improving not only the individual skill but also the number of skills and tools they have available overall. In this way, the coach is building the team's capacity.

As the coach helps the players learn to analyze game situations and as the players improve their decision making, they will begin to understand the choices that they have in a given circumstance, and they will be more flexible and more conscious

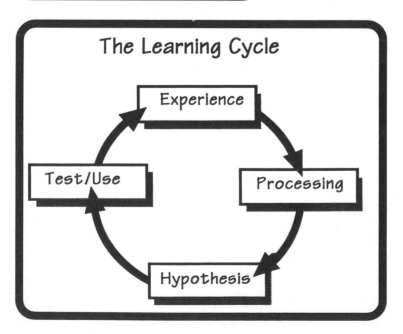

The Learning Cycle

Experience

Processing

Hypothesis

Test/Use

> **FACTOID** In the private sector, there is a clear connection between continuous learning, continuous improvement, and the learning cycle. Ed Demings (Demings Institute, 1999), the inventor of *total quality management*; Stephen Covey (1989), in his book *The Seven Habits of Highly Effective People*; and Peter Senge (1990), in his book, *The Fifth Discipline*, all agree on the importance of individual, team, and corporate reflection as means of promoting ongoing growth and development.

players. They will continue to add deeper and deeper understanding of the game, as well as skills, to their playing repertoire. This is the process of *continuous improvement*; it is also the way individuals gain greater and greater flexibility. More and more people are finding that these same outcomes are achieved in all areas where people are coached to learn from their experience.

There are coaches in business, management, music, and performance, as well as cognitive coaches and teachers as coaches. In each of these areas and many more, it is the coach's job to provide the time, opportunities, and skills to help the client learn from experience. And the very best coaches also help their clients learn to coach themselves.

But often, students in our classrooms or our children at home are reluctant to be coached, and they sometimes ask why coaching is even

> **FACTOID** There is also a clear connection between continuous learning, continuous improvement, and the learning cycle in education as well as in the private sector. For years, Art Costa and Bob Garmston (1994) have been advocating an approach called *cognitive coaching* to foster the growth and development of educators. Donald Schon (1983, 1990), in his books, *The Reflective Practitioner* and *Teaching the Reflective Practitioner*, also sees the connection between metacognitive decision making and outstanding performance.

FACTOID

Long-term memory is truly amazing. It is where we store everything that we learn, and our brains are capable of storing billions of bits of information in neural networks called *engrams*. Our long-term memories have an almost unlimited potential for making neurological connections and for automating tasks and pattern recognition. One of the characteristics of "experts" is that they *automatically* see patterns that novices miss.

FACTOID

Another kind of memory, short-term memory, can hold about seven bits of information at a time. Because this kind of memory can "refresh" itself 18 times per second, it can keep track of a lot. Here's how that works out: $\frac{1}{18}$ of a second × 7 bits = 126 bits of information per second, and that works out to about 7,560 bits of information per minute, and over 70 years at 16 hours a day, that comes out to a whopping 185 billion bits of conscious information in a lifetime. That's a lot!

necessary. It is a good question: Why do people benefit from being coached? To answer this question, students must understand some things about how the brain works. The first thing to understand is that there is more than one kind of memory.

According to learning psychologists, one kind of memory is primarily responsible for holding ideas, concepts, and information for fairly short periods of time while we use that information to solve problems, to figure things out, and generally to think and be conscious of that thinking. This kind of memory is often referred to as *working memory*. In some ways, working memory is a lot like the memory on a computer desktop. When the computer needs certain information, the computer goes to the hard drive and calls up the necessary information so that we can do word processing or some other task. After we work on the document, we must save the changes back to the hard drive. If we don't save that information back to the hard drive and we turn off the computer, that information is lost. The same is true for working memory. It doesn't store information long term; it is simply the place where we call up information from our *long-term memory* so that we can think about it and solve problems.

Automaticity is the term used to describe a person's ability to perform some tasks on automatic pilot. Once some behavior has been learned so well that it can be expressed directly from long-term memory, we can actually do that behavior while thinking about other things. Most people, for instance, have stopped paying attention to their own driving. And they no longer learn from the experience . . .

Long-term memory is where we store everything we learn; faces, formulas, behavior patterns, and emotional responses are all stored somewhere in our long-term memory, in neural networks that are called *engrams.* Because the brain creates these neural networks in an associative, rather than linear way,

FACTOID Computer and neural scientists have been studying the behavior of "experts" for many years in hopes of uncovering patterns of thinking that can be used to develop computer-based artificial intelligence. They have found that many excellent chess players, architects, and teachers tend to automatically recognize patterns and then respond without *consciously* thinking through every option. It is interesting that psychologists like Ellen Langer (1989, 1997) have found that the opposite kind of thinking, what she calls, *mindfulness,* leads to even more astute pattern recognition and decision making. Mindfulness is marked by greater flexibility, more executive control, and generally better outcomes.

one event, one thought, or emotion can trigger another, in a kind of cascade of stimulus and response. What is even more interesting is that these stimulus-response cascades often occur automatically, without any conscious thought at all.

The most powerful aspect of coaching is that it breaks the person's out-of-conscious patterns and brings him or her back to consciousness. Whenever a pattern reaches the level of automaticity, we stop using our working memory for that task pattern. Our behaviors, emotional responses, and decisions emanate directly from long-term memory, they bypass our working memory, and we "do what we've always done, the way we always do it." Coaching interrupts the pattern, allowing the coached person to observe his current experience from a fresh perspective and to actually process the experience in working memory. It is this process that moves people to begin to learn from experience and to make conscious choices about how well old patterns of response and behavior are really working.

The same is true when we think about self-coaching. There is a four-step cycle that provides a framework for learning from experience. Sometimes referred to as the *scientific method*, the *learning cycle* is a method that suggests that we don't learn simply by having an experience. Instead, we must take time out to reflect on and process the data that the experience provides.

Sometimes, we might compare or contrast what actually occurred in a given situation to what we thought would happen. Other times, we might look for cause-effect relationships, or root causes of something that happened in the experience. Last, we might simply ask ourselves the question, "What worked?" to be able to replicate a success.

Regardless of what specific kinds of processing we do, the fact remains that if we are to really learn from our experiences, we must have the time and opportunity for reflection.

Introducing the Learning Cycle to Students

The learning cycle can be introduced to students in a number of ways. At first, the teacher may want to simply introduce the vocabulary of learning from experience and self-coaching. Adults who model their thinking for children can provide useful patterns that children can begin to acquire, just as they do language. The power of modeling probably can't be overstated.

Next, the teacher can begin a formal, and at the same time an engaging, introduction to the four steps of learning from experience. As the teacher begins this phase, there are three outcomes or objectives to keep in mind:

I.   The students should understand and apply the four steps of the learning cycle:

      A. Observe and record experience or data
      B. Process the experience or data
      C. Form a hypothesis
      D. Test or use the hypothesis

II.   The students should understand the importance of observing their own responses as part of the experience

III.   The students should recognize what it means to have the "attitude of a learner"

Those steps might be introduced with a game called *Green Magic*.

Known by various names, Green Magic is a wonderfully brain-compatible way for students to understand what it means to learn from experience. To play, the teacher sends a student who knows a secret signal out into the hall, while the class as a whole chooses an object in the room. When the first student is called back into the room, he or she is able to identify the object as the teacher points to or names various objects in the room. The secret to the game, and a reason not

> Having the *attitude of a learner* is almost the antithesis of automaticity. This attitude recognizes that learning requires questioning what we know, and it also requires thinking about our experiences from a fresh point of view. It recognizes that each hypothesis can teach us something, even if it is true we must continue to explore different avenues of thought. Ultimately, this frame of reference can become a habit of mind that extends to all aspects of a person's emotional and cognitive intelligences.

Green Magic Hints & Tips

FACTOID To make the learning even more fun and to help the students really learn the process, the teacher can provide some false clues in the first couple of rounds. For instance, during round, one touch all the objects (even the green one) with your right hand, then pick up the current object with your left. Some students are bound to observe this and suggest a hypothesis based on their observation. During round two, touch all the objects with the same hand. The students will see that "handedness" isn't the signal, and they will be ready to understand when you point out that when we learn from experience, it is the experience that teaches us. This is the attitude of a learner.

to tell the students the name of the game, is really quite simple: The signal is the color green. When the teacher points to different objects in the room, the target object is always the one right after something green, thus the name *Green Magic*.

To make the learning more powerful, the teacher should help the students see where they are on the cycle. He or she may want to point out after the first round that the students have had a number of experiences. For instance, what was different about the times the student said "no," compared to when he or she said "yes"? In addition, the teacher can also help the students see that their so-called guesses are really hypotheses. Last, after three or four hypotheses are on the table, the teacher might want to point out that even though all the students experienced the same thing, there are a number of possible hypotheses and that ultimately, the students will figure out the right answer by looking for and recognizing patterns in the experience. Then, the teacher repeats the process, another round of Green Magic.

More Green Magic Hints & Tips

FACTOID It is a good idea to set up some ground rules before you begin playing. First, no one should shout out answers. The teacher needs to be able to control the tempo of the activity so that he or she can dissect the process for the students. A free-for-all makes it impossible for the students to reflect on the game itself. Second, the teacher will need to continue to encourage his or her students, and he or she should watch for signs of frustration. The goal is that students have success figuring out the secret. If they begin to be frustrated, make the secret more obvious or tell the students that the game is called *Green* Magic. For the students to develop the attitude of learners, their first experience should be successful.

Usually, students will need five or more rounds before they figure out the solution. During each of the rounds, the teacher should encourage the students and continue to explicate the steps in the learning cycle on an overhead or chart so that students see that they are observing, processing, and forming and testing hypotheses.

The ultimate goal is for the students to apply this attitude and approach to their lives. When students begin to see their emotional lives as a rich set of experiences, they will begin to learn to question themselves and to learn from those experiences. In fact, the very questions they ask represent a set of data that can lead to deep reflection and awareness. What are the patterns? What are the topics and concerns? How do the questions we ask ourselves define who we are? These are the kinds of questions that may never be completely answered, and yet they are the kinds of questions that make us most conscious of what it means to be emotionally literate.

Summary

Learning, whether about emotional literacy or about day-to-day competencies or content, is a result of conscious processing of our experiences and learning from that processing. This chapter introduces the *learning cycle,* a model for this process of learning. It also offers activities that will help students develop the attitude of a learner, using a nonthreatening, fun strategy called Green Magic.

Emotionally literate people apply this same model to all of their behaviors by being conscious of their experience and data, processing that data in an effort to repeat what is useful and change what is not, and then applying the new learning to future behavior.

10

The Power of Vision

Identifying Outcomes

Contents

- Developing a well-formed vision
- Understanding the power of vision in the change process
- Understanding outcomes
- Planning to move from the current state to the desired future

The future influences the present just as much as the past.

—Friedrich Nietzsche

There may be no single factor that is a better predictor of success than having a clear vision of the desired outcome. In our workshops over the past 10 years, with thousands of people, we have found that many people simply do not have a clear idea of their desired outcomes when they engage in the kinds of conversations that could be characterized as difficult. We often go into these kinds of challenging situations with concern and sometimes with a certain degree of anxiety, yet often, we begin these talks without understanding our own interests nor with a clear sense of what a win-win outcome might look like.

An *outcome* is the desired goal or the results of the vision being attained.

A *vision* is a rich description of the preferred future, including what it would look like, sound like, and feel like.

A *mission* is the definition of the purpose for the actions to create or reach the vision.

The Attributes of a Well-Formed Vision

• Future oriented
• Stated in the positive
• Concrete and specific
• Ecological-systemic
• Within the person's influence

Structural tension is created when there is a discrepancy between what we have and what we want. Human systems do not tolerate structural tension and will move to relieve the tension. Some systems relieve the tensions by moving toward the vision; others release the tension by abandoning the dream. The same is true for teams of people, for site-based decision makers, or for individuals.

In addition, there are key elements of creating well-formed outcomes that most people simply have never had an opportunity to learn. As a result of this lack of understanding, those people who do make the attempt to develop a clear vision often end up formulating something that actually *decreases* the likelihood of success.

In this chapter, we will examine the characteristics of well-formed visions, and we will clarify the relationship between visioning and problem solving. To begin, we will examine the importance and power of a compelling vision as a motivator and essential element of change.

The Importance of Vision

A compelling vision of a future desired state is probably the most powerful motivator in the change process. Because of this, creating a vivid vision is almost always the first step in planning for or creating the desire for any kind of change. This is true for a number of reasons.

First, a strong vision creates *structural tension* or dissonance between what one currently has and what one sees as a possibility in the vision. The vision creates a kind of a magnetic pull. Because human systems do not tolerate this kind of tension, we will do something to relieve the stress. Basically, there are two choices.

One of those choices, as described by Peter Senge (1990), is *erosion of goals*. Certainly, we all know people who have simply let go of the vision. Perhaps they rationalize their decision by thinking that the vision was too unrealistic or that attaining it would be too difficult or cost too much time, energy, or sacrifice. Yet once we have had a picture of what could be, the "now box" (otherwise known as the *current state*) never looks quite the same.

The other approach to relieving structural tension is to keep the vi-

> Peter Senge (1990), in his book, *The Fifth Discipline*, describes a number of archetypes of behavior that human systems (as either organizations or individuals) might adopt. One of these is *erosion of goals*. Senge describes this as the process of abandoning goals and visions instead of maintaining the commitment. Over time, erosion of goals becomes a vicious cycle that undermines the individual's self-esteem and his belief that his efforts will make a difference in the first place.

sion alive. Once we have that strong vision, we must maintain it. Effective leaders do this by constantly articulating the vision back to the stakeholders, by talking to people about it, by refining and adding to it as a measure of its vitality. So too, individuals with emotional literacy tend to keep their visions alive by talking to others, by dreaming and imagining, by reminding themselves to take the vision out and look at it. By creating the mental or, for that matter, real picture of the vision, the emotionally literate person keeps his or her eye on the target.

The power of vision can be seen all around us. It's the reason architects and builders sponsor home shows. When these people arrange home shows, they set up real kitchens. They do this so that the visitors to the show will have a concrete and specific vision of their new kitchens; the potential clients will experience what that kitchen would look like, sound like, and feel like. By providing a compelling picture, the home show organizers fulfill the key first step in creating the desire for change. They do this for one simple reason: They know they can't *make* the customer buy a new kitchen. On the other hand, they can create a powerful, compelling vision.

FACTOID Travel agents have begun providing potential clients with video tapes of exotic vacation spots, in addition to the traditional brochures. They do this because the travel industry has discovered the power of a vivid, concrete vision to motivate people to go on vacation!

FACTOID Architects and home builders now have computer programs so that a family can take a 3-D tour of their dream house. The program puts colors and pictures on the walls and furniture in the rooms and even gives people the ability to "walk" from room to room. The reason builders use these virtual tours is simple: They want people to sell their present houses and move out for something that's not even built yet!

Once this "kitchen vision" has been created, it not only creates the mental picture of the desired target that the customer now sees that he or she wants, but it also increases dissatisfaction with the present kitchen. The present kitchen, by comparison, is no longer acceptable. The flaws and problems, the noisy dishwasher, become more obvious, and this actually increases the motivation to get the new kitchen. Not only does the person want to move toward the new kitchen, he or she wants to get away from the present one. The desire for the new kitchen sets up structural tension. If the person should let go of the vision and decide to settle for the present kitchen, the truth is, it will never look the same. People who understand change also understand that a clear, powerful vision is a key to creating any kind of change.

The same is true for all visions. To plan a good party, a person has to have, at some level of consciousness, a vision of what the party should be. What kind of food, music, lighting to have, what time of day or night, what kinds of activities, and even who to invite are questions that can only be answered if there is a vision of the party in the mind of the person putting it together. The same is true for conversations we will have; the same is true for the house we want to build, the relationships we want to create, the work we want to do; the same is true of just about all aspects of our lives. Emotionally literate people recognize and ness the power of vision to guide their relationship choices. And according to Waters and Lawrence (1993), emotionally literate people depend on the power of vision to help shape who they will become as they continue to grow and develop over their lives.

Last, vision helps determine the strengths and weaknesses we possess at any point in time. After all, whether a particular set of behaviors are useful or not is in large part a function of where the person

> Emotionally literate people tend to be successful in many aspects of their lives: at home, at work, in school, and in their relationships. One reason for this is that they are clear about their goals; they create useful visions of what they want to achieve before they begin to act. This is sometimes known as meta-cognition, and it is one form of self-coaching.

wants to go. How does a person even know if a particular behavior should be repeated or discarded if he or she doesn't know what outcome he or she is after? Although this might sound obvious, many people behave as if they don't understand this simple lesson. They go into relationships with people who clearly are not going to support their ongoing growth; they engage in risky behaviors that over time diminish the options and choices they have; they repeat the same mistakes over and over again. Emotionally literate people understand the power of vision, and they use that power to avoid these kinds of mistakes.

But to harness this power, the emotionally literate person must understand what makes a vision useful in the first place. So then, what are the attributes of a well-formed vision?

FACTOID At risk is a general term we use to describe people who are most at risk for making choices that may satisfy short-term outcomes but that ignore the long-term consequences of those choices. People who do not have any long-term vision of their future tend to make decisions that satisfy the here and now. Those with vision are more likely to delay gratification and be more responsible for their short-term choices.

Characteristics of a Well-Formed Vision

In this section, we examine the characteristics that make such an important difference as we work to identify the vision that will shape choices. A well-formed vision has five essential characteristics. Each of these characteristics can have a profound effect. A vision should be

1. Future oriented
2. Stated in the positive
3. Concrete and specific
4. Within the person's influence
5. Ecological or systemic

To foster a better understanding and to support the teaching of these important characteristics, the next section presents each characteristic in detail.

First, then, the vision should be future oriented. Often, when people engage in what they think is visioning, they instead focus on the here and now, describing what it is that they don't like. However, people with high degrees of emotional literacy recognize that dissatisfaction with what they currently have is a signal to take action. Before they take action, they must know where they want to go. A future-oriented vision focuses the person on what the goal state is.

Second, the vision must be stated in the positive. This second characteristic is directly related to the way the human mind processes information. By stating the vision positively, the emotionally skilled person imagines what *will exist in the future.* This is important because the human mind can only imagine the presence of something. This explains why teachers create classroom norms that describe what the students' behaviors should be. A rule like, "Don't run in the halls," is obviously stated in the negative. For a student to understand such a rule, he or she must actually envision running in the hall and then negate the idea of running in the hall. Restating the rule to "Please, always walk," makes it more brain compatible.

The same is true for creating mental visions of the preferred future. Creating a positively stated vision is one of the distinctions that sets the most highly effective people and organizations apart from the rest. Good coaches, good leaders, and emotionally literate people create such visions.

Olympic athletes have coaches. At that level of performance, it is often the mental conditioning that makes the difference in an athlete's ultimate achievement. Clearly, all Olympic athletes follow pretty much the same scientifically determined diets; they have the same kinds of training programs, and they are in outstanding physical condition. The difference that makes a difference, the key distinction between one performance and the next, is the ability to envision the goal vividly and positively. Sports psychologists know that their clients undermine their own performances when they create negatively stated visions—"Don't overarch in the dismount," creates the same cognitive misstep as "Don't run in the hall."

Even though there may be many things in the current circumstances that lead the emotionally literate person to be dissatisfied or unhappy, he or she will use that dissatisfaction as a catalyst to begin asking the questions that focus him or her on what he or she would like things to be in the future. He or she will recognize that there isn't anything that can change the circumstances by focusing only on the past or even the present. Making the vision future oriented focuses the emotionally literate person on the kind of thinking that can make a difference.

The third key characteristic of a useful vision is that it is concrete and specific. What exactly will be happening that is the signal that we can celebrate the attainment of the vision? What is the proof? What would we see, hear, feel? As we examine the third step more closely, we see that it is here that we describe the target state. In addition, by

FACTOID Ever since the Seoul Olympics, where Greg Louganis hit his head on the diving board and then came back to win the gold medal, there have been more sports psychologists in attendance at the Olympics than there have been medical doctors for the athletes. By the way, Louganis has never seen the tape of his accident. He doesn't want to have the mental picture of that dive because he knows how powerful that negative vision could be.

There is a difference between the syntax of language and the syntax of the mind. We can say things in words that the mind can't do. For instance, a person can say the words, "Don't think of a green elephant," and it is a grammatically correct sentence. Yet the mind does not follow the same rules as language seems to. In other words, the only way to understand the sentence, "Don't think of a green elephant," is to do the very thing the sentence says not to do. Positively stated visions describe only what the mind should actually imagine seeing, hearing, and feeling.

A _target state_ is an explicit end point that has specific observable indicators. It is an articulation of the attributes that will prove that the target has been reached.

A _process_ is an ongoing means to attain the target state.

Substituting process for target is a common mistake that many people make when working to create a vision.

Substituting target for process is an error that many leaders make after the work to create the vision has begun.

making the target concrete and observable, we avoid the error of _substituting process for goal._

In this common pitfall, a person will decide that the vision is to "lose 10 pounds." The difficulty here is that _losing_ weight is _a process,_ and _processes can go on forever._ So the person drops six pounds and gains back five. He or she then loses four pounds and gains back two. Over and over, the mind is carrying out the actions to make the vision real—losing 10 pounds, over and over.

If we create a more specific, concrete, and observable target, then we not only have something clear to focus on and aim at, but we also know when we have actually reached the vision. A positively stated vision that is concrete and specific begins to focus our energy, time, and efforts in a healthy way.

The fourth criteria of a good vision is that it should be within the person's influence. There is no point in creating an unattainable vi-

The difference between *control* and *influence* is subtle, but important and it is correlated to the amount of time a person has to affect change. Picture a person at the center of a series of concentric circles. At the center we have control. With each widening circle, the individual's influence becomes weaker and weaker. Now think of time as a square superimposed on the circles. Within the frame of time we have leverage. The more time we have, the larger the square. And this overlap represents our area or scope of influence

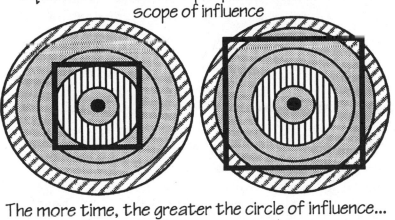

The more time, the greater the circle of influence...

sion. Obviously, there are some things outside of our control, and there are also things that are outside of our influence, but these are really two different matters. Generally, if something is outside of my control, there is nothing, or very little, that I can ever do about it. On the other hand, my degree of influence in a given situation is tempered by time. Obviously, there are things that are outside of my influence if I have only 3 days. Given 3 weeks or 3 months or 3 years, that same thing might be within my influence. If the vision seems too overwhelming, recalibrate the amount of time it will take; after all, visions are supposed to be future oriented.

The last criteria is that the vision should be *ecological or systemic*. As we begin to work with students to help them understand this last criteria, it may be useful to introduce the concept of *congruence*.

Systems thinking requires a comprehensive perspective on the relationship between causes and effects. It recognizes that in complex systems, the effect may not be immediately apparent, and to protect the whole, we must consider all of its subsystems as interconnected and interdependent. If we change any one part, there will be consequences for the others. To be *ecological*, the vision must take into account how the system as a whole will be affected.

Every person is a system; we are really like a constellation of subsystems, parts that are interconnected and interdependent and sometimes in conflict with each other. We have desires, interests, concerns, and fears that influence each other. When we describe ourselves as "conflicted," or "ambivalent," we are putting words to the internal struggles we all have at some time. For a vision to be most useful, the whole constellation, or as much of it as possible, must be aligned or congruent with it.

If one part of the system will be damaged as a result of attaining the vision, the internal turmoil will not only undermine the vision, but it will also disrupt the system itself. For a vision to be ecological and systemic, it sometimes must be expanded to meet the underlying interest of the subsystems. For instance, let's imagine that a person creates a vision of vitality and health that includes running every Saturday morning. If the vision is ecological, then or she or he can feel congruent with this decision. If, however, there is a part of him or her that loves the quiet, relaxed time spent talking with his or her significant other early on those Saturdays, then the running, although a good thing, is not ecological. Moreover, if the loss of that time to talk and reconnect causes damage to the relationship, then the vision will be even less ecological and therefore even less likely to be attained.

To make the vision ecological and systemic, the person would have to expand the vision to include and protect the quiet, relaxed time, talking with his or her significant other early on those Saturdays. As a result, the vision would be inclusive, ecological, and more likely to be realized. In many cases, it is very difficult to reach complete congruence, yet when we at least consider these questions, there are two results. First, we create a stronger, more motivating vision. Second, we foster intimacy with ourselves. We learn to listen and know who we are.

By incorporating the criteria for creating a vision for our future, or for the conversation we will have, or for the way we want to interact with a loved one, we dramatically increase our likelihood of success. We also increase our ability to understand ourselves, our own interests, and what we most value.

Strategies for Fostering Well-Formed Outcomes

Obviously, the first step in this process is understanding the importance and value of visioning. The second step then must be to understand and use the five essential characteristics of a well-formed vision. The third step is to give students guidance and opportunities to use their learning.

There are many ways to incorporate visioning into the students' lives. One way is through writing. Students are taught early on to do something called *descriptive writing*. Visioning can be a teaching tool for something that is already required of students! In addition, journal writing is a great way for students to practice and integrate vision. The journal entries can be focused on either the near or distant future, and they can deal with topics of varying importance. Asking students to envision how they will spend the weekend or what they hope to accomplish as they begin a new project, sport, or hobby is providing opportunities for them to integrate a simple yet powerful strategy.

Students can also begin to integrate a few simple structures that will help them elaborate on and refine their vision statements. One of these structures is a *see-hear-feel chart*. Students simply list details of their vision under each column. They should also be encouraged to develop the habit of mind to ask themselves these kinds of questions in many different circumstances. For instance, "What would I see-hear-feel when I am successful in math?" or "What would I see-hear-feel in a successful relationship with my girlfriend?" or "When I am settled and doing well in college, what will I see-hear-feel?"

Students in cooperative groups can learn that the first step for completing project assignments is to formulate the vision of the completed project. Both large and small, long and short-term tasks, assignments, and outcomes can be the basis for visioning.

Ultimately, the goal is for students to recognize that one of the key distinctions between those people who are successful and those who are not is their ability and habit of creating a clear, compelling vision that can help guide decisions, choices, strategies, and the individual's or the team's focus and energy.

One sign that students have reached this level of integration is when they begin to recognize that it is their role to take responsibility for what they can control, that when something exists in their current circumstance that they don't like, they will be the ones who can make a difference. The first step in that process is to focus on the vision of the preferred future.

Understanding the Nature of Problem Solving

Young people and adults who understand the essentials of visioning also understand that the relationship between the vision and the current state also redefines what is generally referred to as problem solving. When most people talk about a "problem" they have, what they most often do is simply describe what they currently have or what currently exists. And although there may be some implied statement of the different, preferred future, most people never really focus on that aspect of the problem. Instead, they focus on their dissatisfaction with the now box. Certainly, dissatisfaction can help motivate people to change, but without a vision of what would be the preferred future,

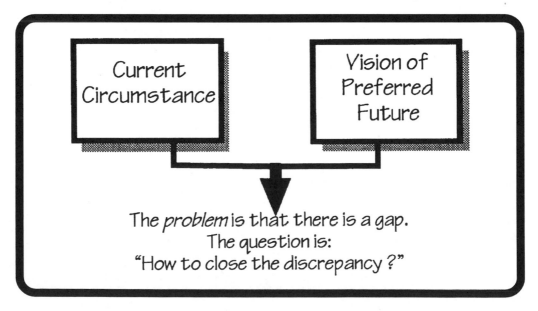

most people end up stuck, simply obsessing on the dissatisfaction they are currently experiencing.

A subtle yet fundamental distinction that the emotionally literate person will see is this: Describing over and over what is in the current state does not in itself constitute a problem. It is simply a description. At the very least, the word *problem* presupposes a possible solution. There is no solution to a description.

No matter how much dissatisfaction a person might feel toward his or her current situation, describing it over and over simply puts the focus on what is. To shift to a problem-solving mindset, there must be some question that can answered. Without the question, there is no problem to solve. And the question will almost always be some form of, "How do I go about creating the future I see in the vision?"

Once we formulate the question, the challenge is to solve it. This is the distinction that the empowered, emotionally literate person understands. Instead of being stuck, focusing on the dissatisfaction with the current situation, the skilled person will follow these four steps:

1. Recognize the dissatisfaction with the current state
2. Formulate a well-formed vision of the preferred future
3. Ask the question, "How to bridge the gap between the current state and the vision of the preferred future"
4. Assess the resources to help realize the vision and identify obstacles that have to be addressed

These steps do not guarantee that the vision will be reached, of course, but it does focus the person or team on action, and taking action increases the likelihood of success.

Here is an abbreviated student example:

1. Help the student recognize the dissatisfaction with the current state.

    Student: I hate not having time to be with my friends. My parents never let me do anything unless my homework is completely finished, even when there is something good to do.

Teacher: What is it that you really don't like?

Student: They don't let me do anything. They are always checking up on me like they don't trust me, and they treat me like a baby, and that is what I really don't like.

2. Formulate a well-formed vision of the preferred future.

Teacher: So what would it look like and sound like if they were treating you the way you want? What do you see happening, and what kinds of things would they be saying, and what kinds of things would you be saying and doing?

Student: Well, I don't know. They would just be better and they would trust me.

Teacher: OK, that's good, but help me to see it so I understand more clearly. For instance, what kinds of things would they and you be saying when you wanted to do something on the weekend?

Student: First, they wouldn't say, "you can't go out until all your homework is finished."

Teacher: Hold on a second, tell me what they *would* say, so that I get the idea of what you *want*, not what you don't want.

Student: All right, they would say stuff like, "We know you have homework this weekend and that there are things you want to do, too. What is your plan for getting everything done?" See, I want them to ask me, not tell. And I would say, "I am going to start Saturday morning and work for a couple of hours, and then I'll finish my math Sunday after the game. If I don't have everything done by the time I usually watch TV, I'll work instead."

3. Ask the question, "How to bridge the gap between the current state and the vision of the preferred future."

Teacher: OK, so what will help you get there? What will you have to do, what steps do you need to take?

Student: I think I would have to tell them that I can do it on my own and that I won't forget if they give me a chance. Also, I probably need to get a plan for doing my homework and maybe even do it first, before I ask them. So, yeah, that's what I would have to do.

4. Assess the resources to help realize the vision and identify obstacles that have to be addressed.

Teacher: OK, so what will help you get there, and what will stand in the way?

Student: I think they might give me a chance, but every time I say I want to do something instead of homework, we start fighting. And then they yell at me, and I get mad and then it's like, forget it.

Teacher: Tell me what needs to happen then so that they'll listen. How can you overcome that obstacle? And what is there that can help you so you get your goal?

Student: Well, I could show them that I have my homework all finished before I ask them. That way, we wouldn't have to argue, and they would see that I could get it done without them pushing me. And I could say, "Let's try it for a couple of weeks to see, and if I don't do it, then we can go back to the old way." But I won't forget, and they'll see, so that would be good. So what do you think? Will it work?

Teacher: To tell you the truth, I don't know; nobody knows. But I do know this: There are no guarantees in life, but if you don't give it a shot, then the only person you can blame is yourself for not trying.

This approach is empowering. It empowers the team, the family, or the individual to create the future. Surely, some future will occur, and the more we teach students to envision and create that future instead of letting it happen to them, the more we enable them to be emotionally literate. They can envision the kind of emotional life that will best provide for their long-term needs.

More important, it shifts the responsibility to the only person who can make a difference, and accepting this responsibility may be the ultimate measure of success.

Summary

The most important driving force in change is a well-formed vision, owned and articulated by the people making the change. Five specific criteria determine the probability of the success of that vision: that it is

1. Future oriented
2. Stated in the positive
3. Concrete and specific
4. Within the person's influence
5. Ecological or systemic

Once the vision is clear, it creates structural tension, a compelling pull toward achieving that goal. A precise "how to" statement is the next step in moving toward that desired state and in beginning the steps in solving the problem or creating the plan for change.

An emotionally literate individual consciously creates a picture or vision of his or her desired outcome and accepts the responsibility for taking the steps necessary for achieving it.

11

Attribution Theory

Foundations of Self-Esteem

Contents

- What is attribution theory?
- Examination of the relationship between attribution and self-esteem
- Explanation of specific attributions and emotional literacy
- Introduction of strategies for enhancing positive attributions

We are all apt to believe what the world believes about us.

—Mary Ann Evans

Anyone who has felt the satisfaction of completing a crossword or jigsaw puzzle knows that the human mind constantly strives to form order out of chaos. In life, we see this process when the mind seeks to link success or failure to specific causes so that it can predict what actions would be appropriate in the future. After all, *it makes sense to find the causes of both our successes and failures if we want to repeat success and eliminate failure.*

The study of how and why the mind links (or attributes) events to specific causes is called *attribution theory,* and the first part of this chapter will examine the psychological foundation of attribution the-

Many researchers have explored the ways that the human mind links, or attributes, causes to effects. By creating these links in time, the brain creates patterns of cause and effect that make the world more predictable and safer. Some of the things that the mind uses to link causes to effects are time, immediacy, and consistency. For instance, if one event occurs just a moment after another, the mind will be more likely to attribute causation than if the events are separated in time.

ory: How does attribution theory give insight into a student's self-concept? How does attribution theory help us understand the dynamics of student effort?

Hunter (1987) presents one of the most interesting and important facts to arise from this field of psychology: it is that a learner's "perception of causality, rather than reality, influences situations, feelings of potency, and subsequent motivation to put forth effort" (p. 96). Thus, attribution theory has important implications for teachers and students alike: *A learner's perception of the causes of past successes and failures has a direct impact on his approach to new tasks or learnings.* The second part of this chapter will examine the implications that attribution theory has for teachers and parents.

FACTOID People generally attribute their successes and failures to these four categories:
• Luck
• Task difficulty
• Innate ability
• Effort

FACTOID People tend to attribute their successes to things they control: talent and effort.
They tend to attribute failure to things outside of their control: task difficulty and luck.

Psychological Foundations of Attribution Theory

A learner's *approach tendencies* are behaviors that a student exhibits as he or she approaches a new topic, task, or area of study. Approach tendencies reflect a learner's belief about what has caused past success or failure. Generally, people attribute (or link) success or failure to four factors:

1. Task difficulty ("I got a 100 because it was an easy test.")
2. Luck ("I brought my rabbit's foot; that's why I got 100 on the test.")
3. Innate talent or ability ("I've always been good in math. I have a math brain.")
4. Effort ("I studied hard and did all my homework; that's why I got 100.")

FACTOID Medical studies are conducted using "double-blind protocols" so that neither the patient nor the researcher administering the drug knows whether the person is receiving a placebo or the test drug. This protocol is designed to eliminate belief as a cause of a particular drug's effectiveness. Researchers do this because they know that if a person believes he or she is getting a curative drug, he or she is more likely to get better.

Each of these attributions has an affect on a student's self-esteem and approach tendencies.

FACTOID *Locus of control* refers to the class of attributions a person might make. *External* locus of control describes things an individual perceives as outside of his or her influence. *Internal* locus of control is for those things that a person perceives as within his or her sphere of influence.

The terms *self-concept* and *self-esteem* are often used interchangeably, yet they really refer to very different aspects of a person's psyche. Everyone has a self-concept; each of our students has an idea of who he or she is and of what qualities he or she possesses. Self-esteem is a positive feeling a person has of him- or herself. So if a person's self-concept is positive, they will have self-esteem. Unfortunately, not all people have self-esteem.

If we attribute success or failure to factors within ourselves (effort and talent), as opposed to "outside" forces (luck or difficulty of task), we see ourselves as the originators of what happens and thus responsible for those outcomes.

If the perceived cause of a failure is within ourselves, we feel guilty or ashamed. Tasks that cause a student to fail because they are selected at an incorrect level of difficulty damage the student's self-esteem, and he or she links this topic, task, or subject to negative feelings. As a result, the approach tendency to similar topics will reflect his or her need for psychological or emotional protection. When a student learns to "hate" a subject or task, he or she is really trying to protect his or her ego by avoiding the topic that "caused" the negative feelings or by attributing the failure to the teacher or the subject itself.

But there are other reasons why attributions that link failure to inability or to a lack of talent are detrimental to future efforts to achieve success in that field. For instance, when a learner becomes convinced that "I have no talent in art," he or she has become resigned that (a) failure in art is outside of his or her control and (b) failure in art in inevitable. Obviously, the only way to protect himself or herself from failure is to avoid art: The approach tendency, if we can call it that, is avoidance. Teachers see the results of students attributing failure to inability every day—when their students exhibit "avoidance" approach tendencies.

On the other hand, a student can come to view *success* in a given subject as a result of innate talent or ability, and this too influences the student's approach tendency. Generally, the student will embrace the topic and welcome opportunities to be involved, but because he or she perceives the success as a result of talent and not effort, the student is more likely to become frustrated when success doesn't come easily. In fact, this student is likely to regard effort as unimportant to reaching success.

If, suddenly, learning does not come as easily as it did before and a student fails, he or she may attribute the change to outside forces. Because effort never played a part in past success, the student is not likely to look to himself or herself as the originator of the present failure. He is likely to attribute the failure to luck or task difficulty.

Last, if the student attributes success to luck, task difficulty, or innate talent, he also learns that he has little or no control over success or failure. In reality, effort is the only factor that the student *can* control and rely on to increase the likelihood of future success. If the student perceives that his success is directly attributable to his effort, then he is much more likely to put forth effort in the future. If the student believes that success in art or math or science or

FACTOID Other cultures attribute success and failure to different things than we do in the West. For instance, in Japan, people attribute success to patience. In fact, there is a Japanese saying, "Success is like a butterfly; if you sit quietly long enough, it may light upon you."

A common error made by many parents and teachers is to praise a student's innate talent or ability. Although it may influence a student in the short term, in the long run, it teaches that talent or lack of talent is the key predictor of success or failure. Yet if we want students to be responsible and to put forth real effort, the talent attribution may not be useful.

Certainly, there are people born with musical talent, but the best musicians are the ones who know the importance of practice.

Moreover, once we begin praising talent, then perceived lack of talent can become a huge barrier to effort. Every teacher has heard some child say, "Oh, I'm not good in math [or English, or sports, or music]. My mom and dad say they were never good at it. We're just not a math family."

English is a result of studying hard, he or she will put forth effort to study.

Therefore, the teacher's ability to help students attribute success to effort has a long-lasting, powerful effect on those students' self-concept and feelings of pride,

FACTOID The concept of high expectations for students is talked about a lot, yet no one ever seems to define exactly what a high expectation is. In our workshops, we define a high expectation as a challenge where the students have a *little bit of doubt* about their ability to succeed but that if they try, they can do it. For most people, anything more difficult will actually shut them down so that they don't really try their hardest.

After all, if the students are sure they can't succeed, what's the point of trying?

their perception of pride, and their perception of their ability to succeed. Clearly linking effort to success will increase the likelihood that students will rely on effort as they approach a new task or new learning.

Considerations for Teachers

First, objectives selected at inappropriate levels of difficulty (whether too easy or too hard) make effort irrelevant. If, however, the teacher selects objectives at appropriate levels, students will perceive effort as the cause of their success.

Second, students are more likely to attribute success to their efforts if they have a sense that effort really does lead to success. One way to accomplish this is to let students know the objective (the product) and how to get there (the process.) As a student might say, "If I don't know where I'm supposed to end up and I have no say in how to get there, I can't see taking the blame (or credit) for where I am." Instead, luck, talent, or ease of the task are the "causes."

A teacher modeling the "correct product and process" helps students to see where they are headed and to connect their efforts to their getting where they are supposed to be.

Third, teachers can influence a student's perceptions of the causes of success and failure through providing specific and immediate knowledge of results. By focusing our statements about success and failure on something within a student's control—that is, on effort—we communicate our belief that the student "can do it."

On the other hand, if we excuse failure, we may be communicating that no matter how hard he or she tries, the student lacks the innate ability for success: "It's OK, Susie, girls don't do well in science." Students deserve to believe that they have ability; otherwise, effort is pointless.

Last, teachers can help students by taking the "I" out of praise and replacing it with "you." When a teacher talks about his or her attitudes, likes, or opinions about a student's work, the student's focus shifts to pleasing the teacher. When a teacher says, "I am really proud of you for _____," the teacher is taking the credit for the success. After all, I may be pleased about someone else's accomplishments, but I can only be proud (or ashamed) of the things I do.

On the other hand, when a teacher says, "Your effort and hard work studying really paid off on this task; you should be proud," she is helping the student attribute his or her success to his or her effort. By recognizing the student's decision to expend effort and by praising him or her for it, the teacher reinforces the link between the outcome and the student's ability to affect that outcome. The way we praise has an influence on student approach tendencies.

Imagine the possibilities of what we could do in our classrooms. We already have students who are "afraid to try" or who "know they can't do it." But we can help those students build a new learning history that teaches them they do have ability and that trying is worth putting forth effort. We can deliberately connect their efforts to their successes and bolster their self-esteem.

Because the attributions we make about what causes our successes and failures are so closely tied to self-image and self-esteem, a teacher or parent's careful attention to the dynamics of these attributions can have an significant impact on a child's belief that his or her efforts will matter in many areas of his or her life. Not only is efficacy an indicator of emotional well-being, it is also key to the kind of self-image and self-concept that leads to the emotional effort that is fundamental to emotional literacy.

Summary

Attribution theory is the study of how the brain links success or failure to some cause and the effects that those links have on future behavior. When students link their successes or failures to things within their control—for example, to their effort—they are developing emotional literacy. Once students understand and believe that it is their effort that determines their successes, their approach tendencies to any new learning or task will reflect this new belief. On the other hand, if students lack this belief, they will attribute their successes and failures to things outside of their control and refuse to take responsibility for the effort needed.

This chapter offers strategies for teachers to consider in day-to-day classroom interactions, which encourage students to develop their own senses of efficacy.

12

Effects of Emotional Literacy

In the 1970s, when he first began his research into the attributes of successful long-term relationships, John Gottman (1995) was pretty much charting unknown territory. The theories on how marriages work and on how to make them better did not have much foundation in sound scientific study. The dynamics of such relationships and the maps that could be used to help anticipate the predictable stages in the journey were simply not documented with any real validity. And the common wisdom of the time was, in many cases, just wrong.

Today, the situation is not significantly different. There are a lot of books out there about how to have great communication and wonderful relationships that were written by people who have been divorced numerous times. There are self-help books that leave people feeling worse than when they started. And there are all kinds of theories and programs that are simply not aligned with current research about how relationships and communication actually work.

But there are exceptions. Gottman (1995) in his research has studied hundreds of couples over many years, using sound scientific methodologies. As a result, he has documented specific indicators that can predict whether a relationship will last. And the predictions are amazingly accurate. What's more, there are specific things we all can do to improve our chances of having a sustained relationship, as well as to improve the relationships themselves. Simple things.

For instance, nonverbal gestures and facial expressions make a huge difference in predicting the future success of how well a couple will do in their relationship. If a relationship deteriorates to the point where either of the two people begins to communicate contempt (either verbally or nonverbally), it opens the door to defensiveness, and then the relationship is really in serious trouble. Also, the ability to maintain a positive (nondefensive) attitude during difficult discussions and the ability to communicate effectively seem to be keys to success. People who have successful long-term relationships are able to mitigate their own responses and to recognize and adapt to the style or needs of the partner. Simply being able to nurture a high positive-to- negative interaction ratio is an attribute of people who maintain their long-term relationships in a healthy manner.

Last, the ability to recognize and appreciate that no one marriage style is the right one and to be able to flex and to negotiate a common satisfying alliance is a simple concept for us to understand, but living it is the difficult part. There is lots of research now that can tell us what we should do but much less that tells us how to do it.

The skills of the emotionally literate person are fundamental to maintaining the kinds of relationships that are nourishing and that continue to grow over time. These skills do make a difference.

In 1978, when Joan Borysenko (1987) first contemplated leaving the Department of Anatomy and Cellular Biology at Tufts University to study what later became known as the *mind/body connection*, few people were looking at the relationship between emotions and health. Since the establishment of the Mind/Body Clinic at Harvard, she and her peers have worked with thousands of people and have established a clear link between emotional well-being and physical health.

The correlation between the ability to manage emotion and the functioning of the immune system are clearly documented. The dangers of helplessness, to have a sense of loss of control, contributes to illness, whereas a willingness to be fully aware, to break the anxiety cycle, and to manage our own emotional resource states contribute to health and even to the likelihood that we will recover from serious disease.

People who maintain long-term relationships actually live longer than those who are alone. Understanding and managing emotional resource states, understanding and using effective communication skills, and the ability to respond to our own inner coaches are fundamental to not only the quality of our emotional lives but also to the quantity of our physical lives.

The strategies that are taught at Harvard's Mind/Body Clinic are essentially the same ones discussed in this book: Reframing, consciousness, greater sensory acuity, managing emotional resource states, anchoring, communication skills, as well as other relaxation techniques for monitoring the inner emotional life and for maintaining a relationship with ourselves, are all a part of Harvard's program.

What each of these areas of research have in common is this: Whereas the emotional environments we create in our homes and classrooms do have significant effects on student learning, the implications of fostering emotional literacy go far beyond the schoolhouse.

There are multiple worlds of change that are our children's futures. Lifelong adaptivity will be the primary survival skill. In reports to the federal government about workplace skills for the next century, in the studies of futurists about the demands of the next two decades, in the studies of successful marriages and family relationships, and even in the research on optimal health, the message is repeated over and over again: We must be emotionally literate to balance the forces of change in the world. It will not be easy to live in the future. Now more than ever before, the stresses and anxieties of change are upon us. If we are to truly prepare students to be successful in the worlds beyond school, we must give them the skills of emotional literacy.

13

Some Final Thoughts

What if we understood ourselves and others in a deeper way? What if all of us were more skilled at determining our goals and creating compelling visions in our emotional lives? What if we were more able to understand each other's underlying interests and find win-win solutions that were both collaborative and fair? What if we all were able to protect boundaries and relationships, if we were able to assert and apologize with grace and integrity? What if we were sensitive to the differences in communication cues across cultures and genders? What if we understood the nature of emotion and could manage those emotions in a healthy, productive way? What if each of us, including every child, could look in the mirror and see someone he or she holds in high esteem?

Would all students get higher grades? Would they work more collaboratively? Would we all make decisions that reflect the wisdom to look at what is best for all of us in the long run? Would all we have more peace?

We don't know. And what does not knowing say about us? Certainly, there will be people who will argue that such a place would be impossible, that there is no utopia. And they are right. And yet, there are many people who have survived terrible, hideous inhumanities who have found a way to forgive, to grow, and to make the world a better place because of their contributions. They have taught us much.

Only through rigor, hard work, and self-control can we ever make these kinds of choices.

The implications and next steps are ours to consider, as are these questions: What if we tried? What difference would it make?

* * *

The real voyage of discovery consists not in seeking new lands but in seeing with new eyes.

—Marcel Proust

We can never discover new continents until we have the courage to lose sight of all coasts.

—André Gide

Nobody made a greater mistake than he who did nothing because he could only do a little.

Edmund Burke

When you have to make a choice and don't make it, that is in itself a choice.

William James

You must do the thing you think you cannot do.

Eleanor Roosevelt

What we experience is shaping and organizing matter into form.

Margaret Wheatley

* * *

"Come to the edge," he said.
They said, "We are afraid."
"Come to the edge," he said.
They came.
He pushed them
And they flew.

Guillaume Apollinaire

Resource A:

Brain Structure and Emotion

Clearly, the brain is one of the most complex structures in all of nature, and trying to understand the *mind* by describing individual brain structures is not only reductionist but also impossible. However, researchers have been able to isolate some of the structures of the brain and have found that some of these structures contribute more than others to particular kinds of emotion response. To begin to understand the current neurological research, we must examine the relationship between emotional responses and the physiological responses in the brain.

The Brain's Structure

The amygdala, hypothalamus, and hippocampus are the central (but not the only) structures of what is known as the *limbic lobe,* an area of brain that is roughly correlated to what MacLean (1990) might call the overlap between the reptilian and paleomammalian regions and the neocortex. The complex interplay between these areas of the brain result in expressions of emotion, fight-or-flight behaviors, and the formation of memory and thought.

The Amygdala

A little almond-shaped structure, the amygdala resides deep inside the antero-inferior region of the temporal lobe and connects the hippocampus, the prefrontal (neocortex) area, and the hypothalamus. These connections make it possible for the amygdala to play an important role in the mediation and control of major affective activities, such as friendship, love, and affection, as well as in the expression of fear, rage, and aggression.

The amygdala is like the central clearinghouse for sensory input to the brain. It is responsible for the initial determination regarding the nature of input. And thus, it is fundamental to self-preservation. Under certain circumstances of perceived threat, the amygdala gives rise to fear and anxiety, which lead the animal into a state of high alert, ready for flight or fight. Heightened perceptual acuity, the discharge of neurotransmitters, as well as a long list of other physiological responses are activated in the anticipation of these survival responses.

In animal experiments, the destruction of the amygdala dramatically alters the animals' behavior. They become indifferent to both sexual stimulation and to danger. On the other hand, experimental stimulus of these structures elicits crises of violent aggression or broad swings of emotional and physiological response. As described in *The Oxford Companion to the Mind* (Gregory, 1987) in experiments conducted by "R.G. Heath, expressions of anguish and despair changed precipitously to expressions of optimism. . . . One patient on the verge of tears . . . immediately terminated the conversation and within fifteen seconds exhibited a broad grin" (p. 528). Humans with marked damage to the amygdala lose their ability to understand the emotional significance of outside stimuli, such as the sight of a well-known person. The subject knows, exactly, who the person is but is not able to decide whether he likes or dislikes him or her.

Sensory stimuli pass through this region, and an intact amygdala acts as the early-warning system organizing an individual's initial response to input.

The Hippocampus

The hippocampus is involved in the formation of long-term memory. When both hippocampi are destroyed, nothing can be retained in the memory. The subject quickly forgets any recently received experience. The intact hippocampus allows the animal to compare the conditions of a present threat with similar past experiences, thus enabling it to help decide if the current stimulus is in fact a danger (perhaps something unknown, unexplainable, or ambiguous) or not. The connection between the neocortex and the amygdala runs through the hippocampus and allows the rational, logical intervention of the part of the brain associated most closely with these kinds of cognitive functions.

If the brain interprets the perceived stimuli as a threat, then the amygdala sends messages to the hypothalamus, the brain stem, and the autonomic systems signaling danger and triggering profound responses in each of these subsystems. This activation can override or short circuit the cognitive functioning of the neocortex. Subsequent behaviors and responses (many of which could be characterized as instinctual) are triggered by the hypothalamus .

The Hypothalamus

The hypothalamus organizes the metabolism of the body. For instance, this region controls body temperature and the production and circulation of hormones, as well as the states of aggression or submission. It organizes mating and sexual behavior, as well as instinctual protective behaviors that can be associated with territoriality.

In another experiment described in the *Oxford Companion to the Mind* (Gregory, 1987), when scientists electrically stimulated neurons in the hypothalamus of

> various animals, the animals show manifestations of rage and
> [they] attack any living thing in sight. A pigeon stimulated in
> this way and alone in a cage behaves as if it sees another bird;
> it circles threateningly around the hallucinated bird, preparing to attack it." (p. 530)

Here, we see the interplay of the response to territoriality.

It is interesting that the hypothalamus does not in and of itself initiate behavior. It is the interplay between the amygdala and the hippocampus that creates a sufficient condition for the activation of the hypothalamus. But once stimulated, the hypothalamus controls the production of hormones that affect every organ of the body. The hormones it controls are taken by the blood to the spinal cord and then to the brain and to every tissue. Thus, this part of the brain, in connection with these other regions, is related closely to the organization of emotion and to the total actions or behaviors related to aggression, fear, and sex, acts that require hormones and their effects on neurons and other tissues.

A Caution

Neurologically, there are no reptilian or paleomammalian structures of the human brain. Reptiles have reptile brains; humans have human brains. At best, the triune brain model is simply that, a metaphor, a model, a story that can help us understand the behaviors that humans experience, both internally and externally. As a model of brain anatomy, it is inadequate. As a metaphor for human response, it is exquisite.

Just as the triune model simplifies a complex system so that we might be able to understand some aspects of it, the current neurological descriptions are just different models that help us see some aspects of the total while obscuring others. And just as the triune model does a poor job of describing the anatomy of the brain, the current neurological models and descriptions of the brain often fail to provide the kinds of insights into behavior that the simpler model affords.

For this reason, it is important to determine the specific outcomes that we want when we decide what model we will present to those we teach.

Resource B:

Recommended Reading

Bocchino, R. (1993). Are you planning the future or fixing the past? *Journal of Staff Development, 14*(1), 50-62.

Byrne, R. (1995). *The thinking ape: Evolutionary origins of intelligence.* New York: Oxford University Press.

Csikszentmihalyi, M. (1990). *Flow: The psychology of optimal experience.* New York: Harper & Row.

Dlugokinski, E. (1997). *Empowering children to cope with difficulty and build muscles for mental health.* New York: Taylor & Francis.

Duval, S., & Duval, V. H.(1990). *Consistency and cognition: A theory of causal attribution.* New York: Addison-Wesley.

Ekman, P., & Friesen, W. (1975). *Unmasking the face.* Englewood Cliffs, NJ: Prentice Hall.

Gordon, D. (1978). *Therapeutic metaphors.* Cupertino, CA: Meta Publications.

Griffin, D. (1994). *Animal minds.* Chicago: University of Chicago Press.

Jacobs, R. (1994). *Real time strategic change.* San Francisco: Berrett-Koehler.

Moore, T. (1992). *Care of the soul.* New York: HarperCollins.

References

Association for Supervision and Curriculum Development. (1996). *ASCD training and development handbook* (pp. 202-206). Alexandria, VA: McGraw-Hill.

Borysenko, J. (1987). *Minding the body, mending the mind.* New York: Bantam.

Caine, R., & Caine, G. (1991). *Making connections: Teaching and the human brain.* Alexandria, VA: Association for Supervision and Curriculum Development.

Caron, J. (1992). *An introduction to psycholinguistics.* Toronto: University of Toronto Press.

Costa, A. (1991). *The school as home for the mind.* Andover, MA: Skylight.

Costa, A., & Garmston, R. (1994). *Cognitive coaching: A foundation for renaissance schools.* Norwood, MA: Christopher-Gordon.

Covey, S. (1989). *The seven habits of highly effective people.* New York: Simon & Schuster.

Demings Institute. (1999). [Online]. Staff@demings.org. Available: http://deming.org/deminghtml/wedi.html [1999, February 28].

Dilts, R. (1990). *Changing belief systems with NLP.* Cupertino, CA: Meta Publications.

Ekman, P. (1997). Facial expression of emotion. *American Psychologist, 48,* 384-392.

Ekman, P., & Davidson, J. (1998). Voluntary smiling changes regional brain activity. *Psychological Science, 4,* 342-345.

Farkas, S., & Johnson, J. (1997). *Kids these days: What Americans really think about the next generation* (a report from Public Agenda). New York: Ronald McDonald Charities.

Fulgum, R. (1988). *Everything I needed to know I learned in kindergarten.* New York: Villard.

Gallup, G. H., & Plump, W. (1995). *Growing up in America: And what experts say parents can do about it.* Princeton, NJ: George H. Gallup International Institute.

Gardner, H. (1983). *Frames of mind: The theory of multiple intelligences.* New York: Basic Books.

Goleman, D. (1995). *Emotional intelligence.* New York: Bantam.

Gottman, J. (1995). *Why marriages succeed or fail.* New York: Simon & Schuster.

Gregory, R. (1987). *The Oxford companion to the mind.* Oxford, UK: Oxford University Press.

Hart, L. A. (1983). *Human brain and human learning.* Oak Creek, AZ: Books for Educators.

Hunter, M. (1987) *Educational leadership.* Alexandria, VA: Association for Supervision and Curriculum Development.

Langer, E. (1989). *Mindfulness.* New York: Addison-Wesley.

Langer, E. (1997). *The power of mindful learning.* New York: Addison-Wesley.

MacLean, P. (1990). *The triune brain in evolution.* New York: Plenum.

Rotter, G. (1998, October). Face it. *Psychology Today,* 34-35, 78.

Rubeck, R. B., & Carr, T. S. (1993). Prison crowding over time: Relationship or density and changes in density to infraction rates. *Criminal Justice and Behavior, 20,* 130-148.

Sagan, C. (1934). *The dragons of Eden.* New York: Ballantine.

Satir, V. (1988). *The new peoplemaking.* New York: Science & Behavior.

Schon, D. A. (1983). *The reflective practitioner.* San Francisco: Jossey-Bass.

Schon, D. A. (1990). *Teaching the reflective practitioner.* San Francisco: Jossey-Bass.

Secretary's Commission on Achieving Necessary Skills. (1990). *The SCANS report.* [Online]. U.S. Department of Labor. Available: http://www.ttrc.doleta.gov/SCANS/scanstxt.htm [1999, February 28].

Senge, P. (1990). *The fifth discipline.* New York: Doubleday/Currency.

Senge, P. (1994). *The fifth discipline fieldbook.* New York: Doubleday/Currency.

Slavin, R. (1989). *Effective programs for students at risk.* Boston: Allyn & Bacon.

Slavin, R. (1995). *Cooperative learning: Theory, research, and practice.* Boston: Allyn & Bacon.

Slavin, R. (1996). *Every child, every school: Success for all.* Thousand Oaks, CA: Corwin Press.

Sousa, D. (1998). *Learning manual for how the brain learns.* Thousand Oaks, CA: Corwin Press.

Tannen, D. (1990). *You just don't understand: Men and women in conversation.* New York: Ballantine.

Tannen, D. (1994). *Talking 9 to 5.* New York: Avon.

Tannen, D. (1998). *The argument culture.* New York: Random House.

Ury, W. (1991a). *Getting past no.* New York: Bantam.

Ury, W. (1991b). *Getting to yes.* New York: Bantam.

Waters, D., & Lawrence, E. (1993). *Competence, courage & change.* New York: Norton.

Index

CORWIN
PRESS

The Corwin Press logo—a raven striding across an open book—represents the happy union of courage and learning. We are a professional-level publisher of books and journals for K–12 educators, and we are committed to creating and providing resources that embody these qualities. Corwin's motto is "Success for All Learners."